RETURN TO GLORY

THE RISE, FALL, AND REDEMPTION OF BARBADOS AND WEST INDIES CRICKET

Grantley E. Edwards

caribbeanchapters

First Edition, June 2015.

Caribbean Chapters Publishing Inc.
P.O. Box 8050, Oistins, Christ Church, Barbados
www.caribbeanchapters.co

ISBN (paperback): 978-151-4671-04-7

ACKNOWLEDGEMENTS

I extend my heartfelt thanks to Morris McCallister who helped me to clarify my ideas. I give thanks and appreciation to Cathy Candace Belgrave for her general contributions and unstinting support.

I sincerely thank former Senior Superintendent Leonard Brome for his help in arranging an interview with his first cousin, Charles Griffith.

Lastly, but not the least, I extend my gratitude to Dr. Daniel Osei-Johene for strongly suggesting that I record my cricketing thoughts in a book.

ABOUT THE AUTHOR:

Grantley E. Edwards is an ardent cricket fan who as a little boy went to bed with cricket on his mind and woke up the next morning with a bat in his hand. He admired Sir Frank Worrell for his cool demeanour, his leadership skills, his intelligence and his diplomacy. He marvelled at the audacity of Sobers and Kanhai. He often wondered as to whether Hunte and Nurse were dancing or batting. Perhaps they were doing both simultaneously. He admired the power and grace of Hall's bowling and sheer power of his partner Charlie Griffith.

Grantley attended All Saints Elementary School and Coleridge and Parry High School in St. Peter, Barbados; both were all boys' schools. He left for England in the early 60s where he joined the British Royal Air Force. He served in the Middle East and Germany. On completion of his service, he attended London University — The Institute of Education, Kings College and Birkbeck College. He completed his Masters in 1981. He taught at a high school in London. He also took up a post of administrator in the said school. He spent his last five years in England lecturing at Newham College of Further Education, London. He returned to Barbados in 2006.

Grantley is also the author of: *An All-African Disease - ENDO-RACIALISM - The Disease of Blacks Everywhere.* This book was first published in London in 2009 under the authorship of Kwaku Grantley E. Edwards by TamaRe House Publications: www.tamarehouse.co.uk

TABLE OF CONTENTS

INTRODUCTION

This book seeks to chronicle the glory days of Barbados cricket from 1960-1990. It starts from the premise that these radiant days gave rise to West Indies' global dominance during this period, and this premise is in turn based on C.L.R. James' assertion. The famous Trinidadian historian and writer asserted that West Indies cricket is Barbados cricket, hence, the dominance of Barbados which was reflected in the West Indies.

This work entirely accepts C.L.R. James' description of the cricketing brand that is defined as Barbadian, and by extension West Indian. He described this brand as an attacking, exciting and attractive spectacle of fast bowling and batting.

It will attempt to show the origin of this brand by identifying the central figures in creating this cricketing phenomenon. The Three Ws: Worrell, Weekes and Walcott, though they took the baton from forerunners such as George Headley, are seen as the founding fathers of the brand.

This account will clearly show how the English game of cricket was brought to Barbados by the Sugar Barons. It will trace the involvement of the African-Barbadians who transformed this game into something new. Using the analogy of the African-Brazilian who transformed English soccer into a game of skill and creativity, this chronicle will show how Weekes, Worrell and Walcott established cricket on a higher plain.

The dissertation is based on the underlying belief that this brand of cricket was superior to all other forms of cricket, and this is the reason why it conquered the world for three decades from 1962 to 1994. The Barbados and West Indies cricketers who carried this brand sat on top of the global cricketing ladder. To play English county cricket, therefore, they had to descend a number of rungs or notches to join these county teams which were of a lower standard than what they had become accustomed to in domestic cricket at home and at test level. Thus it seems illogical to assert that Barbados and West Indies cricket owed their dominance to a 'finishing school' in England county cricket. This would be tantamount to saying that these West Indian cricketing high school graduates had to descend the cricket ladder and attend a primary county cricketing school in England in order to apply the finishing touches to their game.

In any case, none of these Barbados and West Indies cricketing stars of this dominant period adopted an English approach to the game; proof indeed that county cricket, the so-called 'finishing school', hardly affected either their batting craft or their bowling, for by and large they remained true to the brand established by their founding fathers.

Garfield Sobers, Rohan Kanhai, Lance Gibbs and Derek Murray were initially some of the West Indian cricketers that were recruited for the first time to play county cricket in 1968. These were established Test players who introduced the West Indian brand of cricket to the county circuit. In other words, together with those that followed, they were the cricketing teachers in county cricket. Given this fact, it can be asserted that the West Indians provided the 'finishing school' for English cricketers and not the other way round.

For example, county cricketers must have learnt a great deal by rubbing shoulders with Sobers and Kanhai and the many great West

Indian players that followed in their footsteps. Moreover, there was a clear understanding that these luminaries would carry out extra duties in helping young county cricketers. It is not surprising, therefore, that the English cricketing authorities went out of their way to facilitate the entry of these West Indian cricketers to the county circuit, for Sobers at the time was not only considered the greatest all-rounder, he was seen also as the greatest batsman. It must be added that some people around the rum-shops in Barbados considered Kanhai a better batsman.

Lastly, but most importantly, the book pinpoints the main causal factor that led to the fall of Barbados and the West Indies. It gives practical suggestions as to how this brand can be reclaimed from the ashes. It will present a comprehensive action plan to rescue a trademark or a brand that is being buried under a deluge of distorted information, and surprisingly this burial ceremony seems to be a joint venture between West Indian commentators and administrators, together with those abroad who saw the brand as a threat to their dominance.

PART ONE

THE GREAT DECEPTION

Mickey Stewart, the 1963 English opening batsman who later took up the post of England's manager in the late 80s, stated: "county cricket has served as a finishing school for West Indies cricketers." He made this statement in response to the West Indies' total dominance of cricket between the late 70s and mid-90s. At the height of this dominance there were other voices in England crying out about this state of affairs.

A programme on television at this very time sought to show that this dominance was due to poverty. They put forward the central and underlying theme that Barbadians (the programme was based on Barbadian cricketers) in their desperate attempt to overcome poverty, looked to cricket as a means to escape these so-called woeful conditions. Taking on a priori stance, the TV programmers tried to prove their case by interviewing a Barbadian lady who confirmed this viewpoint. After some leading questions and prompting, she stated that cricket would be a means for her son to progress economically. While her statement cannot be wholly dismissed, it is a rather myopic view to seek to explain Barbados' dominance in cricket as due to poverty.

Similar to the Micky Stewart mantra of "an English finishing school", such statements and notions seek to deny the contribution made by Barbadians and West Indians in developing modern cricket. It should be noted that Stewart did not state that West Indians, spear-headed by Gary Sobers and Rohan Kanhai, entered county cricket under a new dispensation. The English county authorities changed the qualification rules and hence in 1968 these cricketing masters and teachers were invited to join county cricket teams to revive a dying game. So much so that Warwickshire, which comprised of Gibbs, Kanhai and Murray together with other locally recruited West Indians, were in some quarters disparagingly and contemptuously called the "black and white minstrel show"(a Euro-American show where whites blackened their faces and supposedly behaved, danced and sang like Afro-Americans).

In short, to emphasise the point, these early West Indian cricketing pioneers were recruited by English county cricket teams. At the time county cricket was in dire need of resuscitation. Sobers jokingly stated that before they arrived on the scene, at many of these county grounds one man and his dog made up the watching public. These West Indian cricketers who led the way were at that time complete cricketers whose batting craft had enabled them to master the swinging ball in humid conditions and the turning ball on wet wickets all around the world, long before they entered county cricket. Kanhai, for instance, before successfully first touring England in 1957, came under the tutelage of Clyde Walcott. Incidentally, Walcott has never played county cricket or even league cricket.

But a fundamental question arises: why would any manager of an English county team patiently and altruistically pay a West Indian while he is learning the art of playing the swinging

CLYDE WALCOTT
Source: espncricinfo.com

ball? Another question that is equally important is this: can a cricketer, at 20 years old, without the fundamental and required skills, effectively learn how to play swing-bowling? Evidence suggests that this is not the case. Doug Walters, a great batsman in Australian conditions, failed game after game in England because he lacked the technique; it was too late for him to master these required skills. Indeed it can be argued that such skills are learnt at a much earlier age; a cross-bat defence cannot change into a straight-bat defence at this late stage. All developmental educational psychologists theorise that such skills are easier learnt at an early age and even if these skills are being learnt at the age of 21, so great is the required effort that the student cricketer concerned can never become a great or even a good player. Late-developing sportsmen tend to achieve only moderate success and by the time, if ever, they acquire the basic skills they are about ready to retire.

However, in the 1950s and 1960s the teachers of cricket across the length and breadth of Barbados, in the villages and in the towns, did not need to read the theories of educational psychologists such as Piaget. They taught, or showed by example, little boys at an early age how to 'play back and across' or 'up and across' as the length of the ball demanded.

Hence great players like Sobers learned how to pick up the length of the ball from an early age. By the time he was 16 years old it had become part of his nature. Yet another important question arises: did the Barbadian players encounter the swinging-ball for the first time in England? Martin Edwards, one of the foremost Coleridge and Parry cricketers of the 1960s, described how he came up against a player from Windward club called Farmer. He stated that the ball was "swinging big" both ways. Roddie Estwick, among other things, was a successful under-19 manager of the team that produced such players as Dwayne Smith. In a heated but affable discussion on the mismanagement of Smith, he stated this: "It is a fallacy to say that Barbadians encountered swing-bowling for the first time when they went to England." This statement supports that of Martin Edwards.

Another question arises: if Barbadian players had to join English county cricket to learn how to play swing bowling, where did they learn how to master spin? A fellow Indian mathematics lecturer at a college in East London described to me his early cricketing experience in India. He stated that as a student at university, no one could persuade him to go to lectures when the West Indies were in town. Their mastery of the Indian great spinners—Chandrasaka, Bedi, Prasanna and before them the greatest of them all, Gupti—was unsurpassed. In fact, possibly the greatest opening batsman of all time, Sunil Gavaskar, spoke approvingly of these players. The greatest of all West Indian opening batsmen, Conrad Hunte, was one of those batsmen he greatly admired. Yet on one of the early CBC morning shows on 100.7 FM, a Bajan sports commentator could boldly state that John Sheppard, playing for Kent, could not fail to learn by sitting at the feet of the English player, Colin Cowdrey.

CONRAD HUNTE
Source: cricketcountry.com

John Sheppard came through the same cricket academy as Conrad Hunte, Belleplaine

(BCL) of St. Andrew. It is amazing therefore that he should have had to wait until he was over twenty, and join Kent, to sit at the feet of Cowdrey in order to learn the rudiments of the game. It would seem that Barbadians of this ilk find it difficult to imagine that a young Barbadian cricketer could sit at the feet of a fellow Barbadian, Hunte, as opposed to Colin Cowdrey of England. And to crown it all Conrad Hunte was a more accomplished batsman than Cowdrey. For a long time Cowdrey existed by using the pad as a bat. Hunte would find such a method of playing demeaning.

Some English players, such as Mickey Stewart, found it hard to accept the superior technique of the West Indian players. Hence, they tried to explain away this phenomenon that is called Barbadian and West Indian cricket; for just as the African-Brazilians—Didi, Guerrincha and Pele among others—transformed the English football into a technical and artistic sport, the Barbadian (at the centre of West Indies cricket) transformed cricket and placed it on a higher plain. The African-Brazilians introduced the bending and the dipping of the ball, playing in triangles and the quick-slow-quick movement on and off the ball. The innovations by Bajans to cricket will be discussed fully in a succeeding chapter. This brings another question to the fore: can a university graduate by sitting in high school classes, make himself into a professor? or put to put it bluntly: can any great player such as Gary Sobers, Seymour Nurse and Conrad Hunte gain a great deal by playing in a lesser league such as county cricket? Can a Barbadian cricketer who is accustomed to playing against a highly-skilled Guyanese team

GARY SOBERS
Source: cricketvidep.com

improve significantly by playing relatively moderate teams on the English county circuit?

Barbadians, immigrating to England in the 1960s, readily came to the conclusion that all cricket in England was of a lesser standard than what they were accustomed to in Barbados. So much so that any team with two or more Bajans became the dominant team. The Bajans, if not directly, were indirectly the masters of these teams. Whether it was the London Transport, the British Army or the Royal Air Force, the

SEYMOUR NURSE
Source: espncricinfo.com

CHARLIE GRIFFITH
Source: crickethighlights.com

Bajans dominated. Hence the Brixton depot of the London Transport could on paper challenge some of the weaker county teams, for most county teams could not beat Empire Club at full strength. This premier cricket club at Bank Hall in Barbados was the home of Everton Weekes, Frank Worrell, Conrad Hunte, Seymour Nurse and Charlie Griffith in the 1960s.

The strength of these club teams gave birth to an all-conquering Barbados team. Not surprisingly, therefore, English touring teams found it difficult to beat Barbados. It should be noted that Barbados beat England in 1959. With fast bowlers Wes Hall, Charlie Griffith, George Rock, Richard Edwards and skilled medium-fast swing bowlers such as the Atkinson brothers and Tony White, Barbados sat on top of the cricketing world. This dominance was underpinned by a superior quality of cricketers at all levels across the length and breadth of the island. Such quality was reflected among the Bajans who immigrated to England. A case in point was the annual match between the British Army and the British Royal Air Force played at Rheindahlen in Germany. The contest was centred on which Bajans on one side were going to defeat the Bajans on the other side. In short, most Bajans, confident in their own ability even at this level, dominated and refused to accept that they, the 'sixth formers', could be taught by 'first formers'. Hence, the story goes that a Bajan cricketer enrolled at the Alf Gover's cricketing school in London. He walked out after one session, claiming that the coaches were teaching "nonsense".

This was the belief that conformed to the attitude of many Bajans at the time: a sense or a perception that much of the English coaching was designed for England and not for Bajans. They opined that they had developed their own 'scientific' method and that this method proved to be superior since, in the real cricketing world, they tended to be heads and shoulders above their counterparts. Sobers' utterences, though not as absolutist or aggressive as the Bajan who allegedly walked out of Alf Gover's school, seem to be in some agreement with this commonly expressed view; the belief being that the Bajan traditional method was as good as any other, if not better. Sobers, in one of his books, stated that he partly learnt his technique as a little boy by carefully observing particular batsmen who had been playing for Barbados. This technique stood the test, for it made him the best batsman, bar none, in the world since the late 1950s.

Sobers mused aloud about what kind of qualification these coaches could bestow on him. In fact, Sobers is the only Bajan that seems to have the confidence and the cricketing wherewithal to critique the English cricket coaching manual. But though I understand this sentiment, I believe that the modern coach should be given a course in how to teach as opposed to what to teach as put forward solely by this English coaching bible. This topic will be discussed more fully in a subsequent chapter.

Returning to the main issue, the 'finishing school', Bajans of this generation did not think that they needed to be schooled in cricket by their English counterparts. So much so that when I first landed in Germany, it was no surprise to find a Bajan in charge of the Royal Air Force team. Keith Simmons, who later returned to Barbados and became a government minister, was the manager, the captain and coach all in one. He epitomised the Bajan man, spreading like a missionary the Bajan brand of cricket. And not surprisingly, another Bajan took over his role on his return to the U.K.

Keith Simmons is a lover of the game, but this new czar, Arthur Waithe, fanatically loved the game. He loved life and the two things he enjoyed doing, playing cricket and dancing. His conversation was all about the fairer sex or about cricket. When he was off duty, he could often be found in the Queensway club in Germany or at a continental bar in Holland. But cricket was never out of his mind. Cricket was his religion and Sobers was his god. Only one thing would seem to upset this smiling figure— if you question his batting technique. He, like most Bajans in England at that time, seemed to have been carrying an invisible banner. It read: I AM FROM BARBADOS, I LOVE CRICKET, CRICKETERS FROM BARBADOS ARE LIKE

ME: THE BEST IN THE WORLD.

This seemingly arrogant attitude, only considered as confidence by Bajans, was buttressed by the realisation that Sobers, the Bajan cricketer, was often on the English TV as a celebrity. In fact, he once appeared on TV with Mohammed Ali, at the time the most famous person in the whole wide world. Sobers ruled the cricketing world while Ali ruled the boxing world, and for the Bajan of Arthur Waithe's ilk, Sobers was only a product and a simple reflection of Barbados cricket. According to this thinking, Barbados produced cricketers like Sobers and himself.

At the county level Sobers was the teacher and the professor at Nottingham. Haynes and others followed, performing vital roles for the counties; they unwittingly became the teachers. My brother, upon arriving in England, shared accommodation with Keith Simmons. He was useless at cricket and very rarely played the game in Barbados, but even he was expected to play for his office team. Consequently, his invisible and yet visible banner had fewer words, unlike that of Arthur Waithe. It simply read: I AM FROM BARBADOS. It did not allude to any cricketing prowess, for he had none. In short, he made up for the lack of cricketing expertise by spreading the 'gospel' of Barbados. He, like Keith Simmons and most Bajans who went to England, both wittingly and unwittingly promoted Barbados, so much so that England became the main tourist market, replacing Canada.

My brother moved to Sussex in 1964 and last year when I saw him in England, he was still using pictures recently taken in Barbados as visual aids to add spice to his lectures. This so-called patriotic duty seemed commonplace among Bajans as was the case with my uncle. My uncle and his friend from school days displayed the common social trait of most Bajans of that generation in England—a calmness and willingness to resolve issues by discussions. They both were employed at the headquarters of the British national postal services, Mount Pleasant.

Most African-Caribbean people during this period encountered difficulties from time to time. This was partly due to being given the status of lowly immigrants and partly due to the world-wide view that any trace of an African appearance was evidence of inferiority. This view was and is also held in the Caribbean,

South America and North America. Some Blacks in Britain at the time understandably responded angrily to these difficulties. Hence, unfairly all African-Caribbean people were negatively labelled as being aggressive. By contrast most Bajans assessed the situation and reacted accordingly.

The CEO at Mount Pleasant suddenly realised that these two Bajans did not fit the stereotypical image of the aggressive black man. Curious, he kept asking them where they were from, for most Englishmen at the time found it difficult to geographically locate Barbados. These two Bajan post office employees, to satisfy the CEO's curiosity, advised him to visit Barbados, the island in the sun. Obligingly, he boarded that flight bound for Seawell Airport. This case is mentioned because it was a very common occurrence, for many of my fellow lecturers visited Barbados because of this social contact. Ask 'Dockey' Chandler, who set-up a small company providing a plumbing service, of the role he and other Bajans played in getting their customers or workmates to visit Barbados. The mentioning of such cases seems more apt, for some Bajans used this social interaction to promote their brand of cricket and send or accompany these English-based teams to Barbados.

A case in point is that of Mr. Keith Hurst, formerly of Walkers, St. Andrew. He coached cricket in Essex. Naturally, some of these young players were part of a team that visited Barbados in the mid-80s and interestingly his nephew, who later played for Derby County, was among these sporting tourists. Hence Bajans at all levels were carrying out their missionary activities in spreading their kind of cricket and adding to the tourist product.

In general, the mass migration to England, therefore, had intended and unintended spin-offs. At the time mostly young men were recruited here in Barbados to join the British army, to be bus conductors on the London Transport buses and to be station guards for the London Underground (trains). By the late 1960s, many of these workers had become bus inspectors, managing the timely running of the buses and ensuring that the fares were collected. On the London Underground, some became station managers and in some cases managers of a group of station managers. Buoyed with this relative success, they began to set-up social (Bajan) clubs, to sit on school boards and to enter local politics. From this position, they became even more successful in promoting 'brand Barbados', the Barbados brand of cricket and a Barbados as an ideal for tourists. Thus, Barbados has become the place to visit for most English people and a place for cricket tours.

At this juncture I will digress from my central theme to make an important point. My brother attended Coleridge and Parry school, for at the time most boys from St. Lucy, St. Peter, St. James and St. Thomas aspired towards getting a place in this school. He later attended Harrison College. Frustrated with the lack of a career pathway, he left for England in the 60s. He is typical of a country boy from the north of the island. Disciplined, he set himself a number of goals, and he devised a strategy to achieve these objectives. Not easily frustrated, like most Bajans who left during this period, he displayed a kind of patience, tenacity and calmness, and most important a self-belief that he would succeed in the long run. As already stated, these were the characteristics that were common among Bajans of this generation and this gave them the ideal temperament for the game of cricket. This is one of the main reasons why Bajans took to cricket like a duck to water, succeeding and excelling at this game as opposed to other sports which are based on the 'now'—instant gratification.

This generation which produced so many great cricketers believed in self-help and 'make-do'. They were determined to find an area to play, be it a rocky piece of open ground or a road between houses. Because of a lack of resources, they would organise the clubs in such a way that pads and bats could be shared by members. These characteristics allowed them to at first survive and then to move forward under testing conditions in England. A case in point is a lady who had recently arrived from Mile-and-Quarter. She walked to work instead of catching the bus in order to save money to send to her little daughter back home.

These Bajans held fast to their identity which they reasoned has served them well; so much so that they stamped this identity on their children, who in turn also identify with Barbados. Visit their homes in England and most likely you would see maps of Barbados together with pictures of the West Indies cricket teams (1963 and 1966) hanging on the walls. Hence, they are sometimes disappointed on return to Barbados to find, as they perceive it, an island without discipline with the occasional shooting, for their common boast in England was that such behavioural patterns were not part of the Bajan landscape. They had harboured thoughts in England that such things happened in other countries or islands, and not Barbados. They are disappointed further by what they perceive as a 'here and now' society—an island where students wait half-an-hour for a bus to take them to school a stone's throw away; an island where parents drive their children to a school that is situated on their door step and they do this in the name of a so-called middle-class lifestyle. Bajans of this disciplined generation are adamant that this perceived decadent lifestyle is the central reason for the 'fall' of Barbados and by extension West Indies cricket. A society decaying around the edges is giving rise to a decaying cricket culture, according to this thinking.

My brother invited me to his garden party in Sussex sometime in the mid-1980s. At this party was a lady who was a member of the British diplomatic corps in Barbados. She spoke highly of the island, and I suppose this praise made him happy, for most Bajans in England like to think of Barbados as a heavenly place. But here is my most important point. The diplomat described a party held at her residence in Barbados. Among the guests, in particular, were two Bajans. Intrigued, she listened to their conversation. She said that for hours they talked about cricket. They had remembered all the minute details about a cricket match that was played two days before. They could remember almost every ball that was bowled on the day. For these two Bajans, however, the main conversation involved a debate about the tactics the various bowlers used and the ability or lack of ability of a batsman to cope with a hostile fast bowler. As the debate went on, one of the Bajans, with a slightly raised voice, insisted "man he set the wrong field" (for the batsman). Here is a most important point as demonstrated by this debate between the two Bajans. They were passionate and knowledgeable about the game and they carried this everywhere, to England and beyond.

This intense love for cricket took Barbados to the top where professionalism alone could never have taken them. Like missionaries, they promoted and played the game. As already stated, this role was not unusual, for Barbados was carrying out this missionary role since the early 1960s. For instance, the Australians invited Hall and Sobers to perform this service. Denis Lillee, the famed Australian fast bowler, spoke of the occasion when he first saw Wesley Hall bowling—"sheer pace and power," he said. "I want to be a fast bowler like Hall." Then he laughingly began to imitate Hall's actions. Ian Chappell, a great Australian batsmen and astute commentator, spoke about Sobers. "The best batman I have ever seen," he said. And who can disagree with this statement? Sobers, without a helmet, mastered the same Lillee, even though he, Sobers, was in his autumn years. This 250+ against the fierce fast-bowling of Lillee, according to Bradman, was a masterful innings. Sobers was also a master of spin-bowling on uncovered and wet wickets. He also expertly played the swinging ball in England even though the weather was far worse than it is today; for in those days no concerted effort was made to protect the

WES HALL
Source: cricketweb.net

atmosphere from traffic pollution or smoke from chimneys.

Only Viv Richards could match Sobers's ability to play fast bowling and only Lara could match Sobers's ability to play spin. Neither Richards nor Brian Lara could combine these skills—the playing of swing, pace and spin—like Sobers. He, like no other, was an expert in mastering all types of bowling, whether it was spin, fast-bowling or swing-bowling. Sobers became the greatest player because of his love and passion for the game. Reading his biography, one learns that he spent every minute of the day playing cricket as a little boy. This passion was not restricted to Sobers, neither was it so much an individual phenomenon. Boys from communities all over the island wore this passion on their sleeves.

VIV RICHARDS
Source: caribbeanceo.com

They lived and breathed cricket. It was amazing to some and irritating to others when they took their obsession with cricket into a place where they should be dancing to soca, reggae or soul. The Bajans were seen as quaint, preferring to stand in a corner discussing the intricacies of the game.

That aside, I return to my central theme of the glories of Barbados cricket and its true relationship with English county cricket.

The important issues that have to be addressed are: why did English players such as Mickey Stewart make biased statements and more importantly why do Barbadian commentators and players repeat his mantra of "a finishing school in England"? The answer seems to lie in Franz Fanon's dictum: "The Black man enslaved by his inferiority and the White man enslaved by his superiority alike behave in accordance with a neurotic orientation." In other words, Mikey Stewart can only see the English county as a school to improve the West Indies, and not more importantly that the West Indian cricketers went to England to revive and add a new dimension to the game. They were the masters and teachers who revived the game, raised it from its death bed and established it at a higher level.

On the other hand, Barbadian cricketers and commentators unwittingly mired in this inferiority complex repeat, ad nauseam, the mantra of Mikey Stewart. Their experience and research tell them otherwise, but they ignore these experiences and the evidence, for so powerful has this message become that it has drowned out their own history and experiences. Hence the history of West Indian cricket is now being written by non –West Indians or by West Indians who unthinkingly repeat their opponents' view-point. This history does not record their experiences of carrying county cricket on their backs. Neither does it chronicle the destruction of many emerging Barbadian talented players—this destruction caused by playing county cricket in England. Such important historical information is drowned out by the incantation: "the English county cricket educated you." But the county experience, if at all, is so insignificant in the grand scheme of things it should be place as a mere footnote in history. By contrast, the main historical text must chronicle the great contributions the Bajan and West Indian players made to England in particular and the world as a whole.

At this point it is necessary to make a more cogent and coherent case against the narrative of the benefits of county cricket on Barbados players; a case to support the unequivocal statement that this mantra of a 'finishing school' only merits a short note in passing. This new narrative will seek to demonstrate that in over-stressing these so-called benefits, one undeniable fact is overlooked or ignored — English county cricket was the seat of ruination for many a Bajan player. Contrast this ruination with the fact that Weekes, Worrell, Walcott, Nurse, Hall, Griffith, Sobers (only in his autumn years) and Hunte, never played county cricket. Yet they mastered the game and had relatively long, successful careers.

THE RUINATION OF
YOUNG BAJAN PLAYERS

In the mid-1970s, the greatest batsman of the last sixty years, Gary Sobers, spoke to the English press. Gary the greatest, according to Ian Chappell, said that the prospect for the West Indies cricket looked rosy. "There are two young fast bowlers," he said, "who will dominate the scene: Michael Holding of Jamaica and Gregory Armstrong of Barbados." Jamaica kept Holding at home and he did not play county cricket until he was coming to the end of his Test career. Holding went on to bestride the world like a colossus. On the other hand, Armstrong went to Glamorgan at a tender age and fell off the cricketing cliff. Similarly Bourne, according to the English press, made England under-19 players look like mere infants.

Warwickshire recruited this promising Barbadian fast bowler. Bourne faded. He played for this county for a while and then disappeared from the county scene. This was not a happy ending for a cricketer that had such potential. Elcock, according to reports from one of my brothers back in Barbados, was a star in the making. Having heard such favourable reports, expectations were high that this player would follow

MICHAEL HOLDING
Source: mid-day.com

in the footsteps of a long line of Bajan fast bowlers. Elcock, after playing in England, returned to Barbados 'encased in plaster of Paris'.

The greatest of them all, the late Malcom Marshall, was in danger of having to retire prematurely. Bowling for Hampshire day after day took a toll on him. Consequently, he developed back troubles. He travelled around the world looking for a remedy. As a last resort he visited a specialist in Barbados who solved his problem. Joel Garner's experience at Somerset seems to indicate that the unreasonable expectations and work load placed too high a burden on the shoulders of West Indian cricketers, for in his book he described the difference he encountered with the Somerset

JOEL GARNER
Source: cricketdawn.com

management over this issue. In short, the much touted 'finishing school' might be an apt description after all, in that it prematurely finished off many aspiring and potentially great Bajan players.

PART TWO

THE MAKING OF THE GREAT BARBADOS AND WEST INDIES TEAM

There is another and similar school of thought which maintains that the English experience made good Barbados and West Indies players into great players. This school does not subscribe wholly to the theory of the 'finishing school' but nevertheless gives prime and place to the English 'experience' as the reason for the West Indies dominance. However, I would like to quote and examine some of Imran Khan's utterances. These statements tend to point in an entirely new direction. This new path or direction should help us to find a credible answer to the conundrum.

Imran Khan was the doyen of Pakistan cricket. As a captain in the mould of Clive Lloyd, he brought them success. He was a product of Cambridge University who plied his trade as a fast bowler on the county scene and, as such, his statements must carry some weight.

On his first tour to the West Indies, he was bowling in Barbados. According to him, Sobers was looking on and made the comment that he, Imran, was not a real fast bowler. Sobers made this comment based on the plethora or 'glut' of local young Bajan fast bowlers. By comparison, Imran was a medium-to-fast bowler. In response to this comment, Imran incorporated a jump as part of his delivery stride to increase his pace. Sobers' statement and the accompanying response by Imran Khan spring from an implicit acceptance that the standard in Barbados was at the very least as good as that on the English county circuit. Even more important is the inference that can be drawn from an article that appeared in a prestigious English newspaper. Imran in this article compared Pakistan's domestic cricket with that of the West Indies. He described the organisation of cricket in Pakistan whereby teams are organised and run from business centres. For instance, Pakistan Air Lines (PAL) would have a team and similarly a Pakistan National Bank would have a team to represent that particular bank. When such teams met to compete, it was a low-key affair. It lacked intensity and such 'friendlies' tended not to truly test the mental capacity and the cricketing technique of players.

He contrasted this situation with that of the regional competition in the West Indies. He cited, as an example, a regional match— Jamaica playing against Barbados. The proud Jamaicans were there to win for Jamaica while the equally proud Bajans were there to defend their reputation and tradition. The result was a high intensity game akin to a Test Match. Such games tested the mental strength and cricketing techniques of players. Imran was suggesting, wittingly or unwittingly, that this was the experience that made the West Indies great. And it should be added that, by implication, such Caribbean experiences created the dynamics for improving the players' cricketing technique, and by comparison the English experience paled into insignificance.

A case in point would be that of Carlyle Best, the Bajan batsman. He successfully confronted the Jamaican fast bowling trio of Holding, Walsh and Patterson. This positive experience certainly would have strengthened or tested his mental resolve and his cricketing technique. Consequently facing up to Botham of Somerset and England in a Test Match became 'child's play'. A bouncer in this case became a mere long-hop to be dispatched disdainfully into the stand to the delight of the fanatical followers of cricket at what they lovingly called the Mecca, Kensington Oval. In a similar vein, Marshall of Barbados would have had to think long and hard about how to dismiss Lloyd, Kallicharan and Federicks of Guyana in a regional match. Hence, he would have thought of new deliveries to add to his armoury, such as the fast off-cutter. According to Sobers (December 2014 edition of Line and Length) he advised Marshall on how best to introduce and master this delivery.

There are two important points that have to be emphasized at this stage. Firstly, Malcolm Marshall, in playing regional teams like Guyana, was forced to think of different strategies to dismiss such accomplished batsmen, whereas on the English county scene, in playing average teams like Essex, he could 'relax' and still be successful in taking wickets. In fact, it seems natural for him to 'relax' in such games, given the long season ahead. And secondly, as is often the case, credit is given to the so-called 'finishing school' for Marshall's development in producing such deliveries, and sadly no mention is made of Sobers' contribution in helping in this respect. Moreover, no credit is given to the Jamaican, Michael Holding, with whom Marshall was berthed on many a tour. A particular incident occurred, for all the cricketing public to see during Marshall's first Test Match in England. This incident clearly showed that Holding was mentoring Marshall. The feared Guyanese fast bowler, Colin Croft, was declared unwell for this Test Match and Marshall replaced him. Holding noticeably stood at mid-off when Marshall was first introduced into the attack. Marshall bowled a ball which to most batsmen would appear to be slightly short of a length and hence, according to the coaching manual, the batsman is required to play back and across. Boycott, the doyen of English opening batsmen, followed this accepted text-book approach and played

MALCOLM MARSHALL
Source: allaboutwhathappensnext.wordpress.com

back. Unaware that this young fast bowler was more than special, he expected the ball to hit the middle of his bat. Not so, for the ball kicked off the wicket faster than anticipated and at the same time it moved away from Boycott. Marshall screamed: "How's that!" The umpire said "not out." But Marshall was adamant that he had the darling of the English fans, Boycott, caught at the wicket. Extremely disappointed, he truculently stamped his feet into the ground.

Holding, matured and experienced, instantly went over to the young Marshall and briefly had a conversation with him. Holding had seen it all before, for some time previously he had a similar experience in New Zealand. Marshall, after this timely intervention, walked calmly back to his mark and consequently produced an excellent spell of bowling. Holding remained at mid-off casting a watchful eye on Marshall and most likely continued to give words of advice and encouragement. Marshall ended up with four wickets while conceding just over 30 runs, an excellent return for an excellent spell of bowling. But mired in the mind-set, as identified by Franz Fanon, the Bajan narrators subconsciously ignore the contributions of the likes of Holding and Sobers while giving undeserved fulsome praise to the 'English experience'.

In passing, it is interesting to note that Holding, on his first tour to England, destroyed the English Test team with 'pace like fire'. On subsequent tours he also skilfully used the deliveries that moved off the wicket into and away from the batsman. This 'Holding-type' bowling had become an integral part of West Indies fast bowling armoury, so much so that Brian Johnson, the English commentator, at the end of the tour in which England was 'black-washed', said to Richards: "you have beaten us fair and square, but you did not bowl many bouncers." Richards replied: "the pitches were soft and hence bouncers would be ineffective [a ploy to reduce the potency of the West Indies fast bowling attack]. We pitched the ball on a good length and moved it off the wicket."

Such statements are important and should be brought to light in the ongoing debate, for in so doing certain myths are dispelled, one of these myths being that West Indies destroyed England in the 1970s, 1980s and early 1990s by solely using bouncers; the 'use of brute force' is the mantra. Again such myths are designed to hide the fact that these bowlers were skilled.

They were the finished products who could move the ball off the wicket, get the ball to lift from just short of a length or swing the ball in any country, unlike bowlers like Botham and Hadley. They were effective in all conditions, so much so that they excelled in India where even great Australian fast bowlers like Lillee found it difficult. But most important in forwarding this polemic, the bowling craft of Holding, if only by association alone, must have been a major influence on bowlers such as Marshall.

THE BAJAN EXPERIENCE

This polemic has sought to dispel the mantra that the 'English experience' was the vital factor in the development of cricket in Barbados and by implication the West Indies' rise to power. The regional tournament has been duly considered as a major factor, and this cricket competition is being accepted as a credible reason for the dominance. But in putting forward this singular view—that the strong inter-regional cricket experience led to an equally strong Barbados and West Indies team—would suggest a mono-causal approach to historical events. In other words, this approach would imply that this regional competition was the one and only reason for the dominance. This method of a singular cause must be rejected and in its place a multi-causal approach will be followed. This means introducing another cause, possibly even a more important cause than that of the theory of the decadence among New Bajans as put forward by the 'traditional' Bajans or the cause of the strength of regional cricket; this newly introduced and additional cause being the strong local Bajan cricketing experience (which also gave rise to the West Indian experience) and the subsequent melting away of this experience that led to the 'fall'. However, in defining this experience and its derived cricketing craftsmanship, the narrative must be placed in a wider historical context.

BARBADOS, THE CENTRE AND HOME TO CRICKETING MASTERS OF THE WORLD

My uncle, Douglas Worrell, is fond of telling me that West Indies or Barbados cricket did not start in the 1970s and 1980s. He rightly pointed out that many masters went before and that West Indian players were great long ago and long before they started playing county cricket.

But other problems, external to the game itself, prevented their rise to dominance. Before giving an account of the rise of Barbados in the cricketing world, it seems necessary to dwell on some of the external forces that worked against Barbados and the West Indies. Obviously, there were also internal non-cricketing forces that hindered the rise to dominance: social class, regionalism or 'tribalism' and racialism plagued Barbados cricket for a long period, and these were forces that were detrimental to the development of the game. In other words, the game was dominated by two parishes, Christ Church and St. Michael. Hence there was regionalism whereby these particular regions had pride and place over the other parishes. In addition, the school which the cricketers attended largely determined their class and this was a criterion for selection.

This petty and ugly social class structure is a crude copy of the British system and hence is seen as natural as breathing to the Bajans. Thus, it was claimed that if you attended Lodge or Harrison College you would be middle or upper class and merit selection in the Barbados team. The overwhelming majority of Bajan people are classified unexplainably as working class and only one of the nine premiere clubs, Empire, accepted cricketers from this class. The society, to prove that it was more English than the English, placed people in social ranks; deference became the order of the day. Thus cricketers from outside the parishes of Christ Church and St. Michael and who were also of the so-called working class could, only with the help of an 'uncle' join one premiere club— Empire. The so-called middle-class, dependent on government patronage, looked down on the workers who created the wealth while they looked up with meekness to the white ruling class.

Hence, this so-called middle-class had their exclusive club—Spartan. And not surprisingly, this club tried for some time to block Empire, the so-called working-class club, from gaining first class cricketing status. Moreover, race played a major part in selection, for almost all the prestigious clubs were white. Race was so important that even a special stand, the George Challenor, was reserved for whites. Given this social class and racial structure, not surprisingly, the captain of the Barbados team had to be white. Everton Weekes, the working-class hero, was the first African-Bajan captain. Apparently he was so good that it is said that Peter May, the English captain of the 1959 tour to the West Indies, copied the Bajan hero's tactics which he employed in the match, England vs Barbados. All of these factors militated against Barbados cricket in that players were not always selected on merit for the Barbados team. If you were from the north or east and from what was deemed the working-class, selection became a distant dream. But let me turn to some of the external forces. Some of these were obvious and some not so obvious; some were intentional and some unintentional.

As already mentioned, one external factor that operated against Barbados was the over-working of their fast-bowlers in county cricket. This was probably done unintentionally, for from an English point-of-view it was reasonable to expect sterling service from your number one fast-bowler, who was recruited from abroad, to bowl out the opposition. The unspoken contract or understanding being that the payment was in exchange for this unstinting service. Such an understanding of expected hard work seemed to have put an early end to Wayne Daniel's test career. He went to England in the mid-1970s to represent the West Indies in an under-19 team.

WAYNE DANIEL
Source: espncricinfo.com

The English press described him as a man bowling to mere beginners. He quickly made the West Indies team in 1976. So fast was Daniel that the greatest ever English fast bowler, Fred Truman, described him as faster than Holding. Daniel became the work horse at Middlesex and lost that shearing pace and eventually his place in the West Indies team. Wayne Daniel mirrored the history of Vanburn Holder who went to England as a fast-bowler and who resorted to bowling medium pace, concentrating on line and length. But these situations, as already stated, can be seen as having unintended consequences due to the relationship between pay and performance.

In short, if a sportsman is being paid, it is reasonable for the management, in return, to expect hard work and a series of excellent performances. However, there were many clear and unmistakable devices used to stop the rise and the triumphs of the Barbados and West Indies cricket team. Such schemes or devices have a historical context.

The game of cricket is traditionally the game of the ruling class in England and, by extension, the rulers of the British Empire. This was their game which they took to their overseas Dominions and Dependencies. Hence, to lose at this game was symbolic of losing the Empire or at least a dangerous indication that the rulers of the Empire had feet of clay. Not surprisingly therefore, there was a refrain which stated that England would prefer to lose a battleship rather than a Test Match. Hence, according to Truman's account, the unofficial motto of the English team that toured the West Indies in 1954 was the Lord Nelson's saying: "England expects every man to do his duty." It is within this context that rules were constantly being changed to stop the West Indies from winning; for such a triumph is considered, wittingly or unwittingly, a challenge to the English teacher and master who originally introduced the game to his colonial children and underlings.

It is within this mindset that England changed the rules overnight to prevent a crushing defeat at the hands of the West Indies. The bowling of Ramadin and Valentine led to a West Indies series-win in 1950. Ramadin, the Trinidadian mystery spinner, again in 1957 threatened to humiliate the English batting. In the first innings of the first Test Match, they were bowled out for less than 200 and forced to follow on. Overnight, they changed the LBW rule to stop the West Indies in their tracks. May and Cowdrey, due to this arbitrary changed rule, were allowed to use the front pad primarily as a method of defence. Thus Ramadin struck their pads a thousand times and the responses from the umpires were always the same: "not out, old boy!" The West Indies, as a result, wilted and lost the series.

Consequently, the West Indies resorted to the Bajan method of attack, fearsome fast bowling. The English cricketing administrators then proceeded to change to the front-foot rule to blunt the West Indies attack. Yet, the West Indies, taking this device in their strides, effectively continued to use a four-prong pace attack in the 1970s, 80s and 90s. They totally dominated international cricket during this period. Again, the rules were changed to that of bowling only one bouncer per over. It is interesting to note that various strategies to reduce the power of

West Indies cricket continued to be employed until the 'fall' of the West Indies.

Of course detractors of this narrative will counter by saying that this is all a conspiracy thesis. But the social climate at the time suggests otherwise. In the 1980s the English press was stating that the pitch should be lengthened, for the West Indies fast bowlers were taller than previous generations. They constantly complained of short-pitched bowling by the West Indies. Tony Cozier, the famed Bajan commentator, remarked in the English broadcasting press box that Botham was bowling many more bouncers than any one particular West Indian fast bowler. The commentator replied that Botham was not a fast bowler, to which Tony Cozier responded by asking if only medium pace bowlers should be allowed to bowl bouncers. The truth is that the West Indies found no difficulties in dealing with the short-pitch stuff.

However, since the English batsmen found it difficult, this type of bowling became a cricketing problem. They introduced the rule that only one bouncer could be bowled in any one over. They complained, further, that the four-pronged fast bowling attack, with long approaches to the wicket, was slowing the game down. The West Indies replied that they won the games in three to four days and therefore time was not a factor. In any case England had previously slowed down over-rates, as a tactic to avoid defeat. This, for example, was done in the 1968 tour to the West Indies. Not surprisingly, a rule for 90 overs a day was introduced, hoping that this would force the West Indies to play a spinner in order to get these amount of overs bowled in one day. This rule remains in place, but it is of great interest to note that with the 'fall' of the West Indies, the rule of one bouncer was relaxed.

Yet the most destructive intentional or unintentional move against West Indies cricket went unnoticed. Johnathan Agnew, a former English fast bowler who became a cricket commentator, remarked from the press box that Richie Richardson was a gentleman and would be a good candidate for the West Indies cricket captain. It came to my attention at the time that this statement was a master-stroke; it divided up the West Indies into warring factions, for the Bajan, Desmond Haynes, was Vivian Richards' vice-captain. He was the rightful heir to take over on a long-term basis. Haynes, an accomplished player and most astute captain, was passed over for the Antiguan, R i c h a r d s o n — this appointment seems to have created the situation of the Antiguans against the Bajans. Agnew, by this very statement, had driven a wedge into the already

DESMOND HAYNES
Source: espncricinfo.com

existing inter-island cracks. He had succeeded in this endeavour of divide and rule or moreso in this case, 'divide and destroy', for the English press had long before been advocating the splitting up of the West Indies team into its island component parts. But the question still remains as to what is the true nature of Barbados and West Indies cricket.

C.L.R. James, the Trinidadian historian, in his book *Beyond a Boundary*, asserts that West Indies cricket is Barbados cricket. Gary Sobers seems to agree with the Trinidadian when he stated that when Barbados cricket is strong, West Indies cricket is strong. In other words, West Indies cricket is a reflection of Barbados cricket. Hence the experience of playing a high standard of cricket in Barbados should be reflected in an equally high standard of cricket at the West Indies level.

At this stage it is important to describe and reflect on the true nature of that experience and brand of cricket that is defined as Barbadian. An analysis of its origin and its development should give an insight and an understanding of this phenomenon.

Barbados has a long cricket history. Cricket was the sport of the English middle-upper and upper classes. These classes became directly connected to Barbados as it became the main nodal point of the English slave trade. Together with the introduction of cane-sugar production, this trade resulted in creating enormous wealth for the English ruling classes. According to Drayton, the Oxford professor, it initially created the wealth on which the Empire and the British industrial revolution were built. This mirrors the thesis of Eric Williams. Due to this sugar plantation economy, a section of the ruling English Upper-middle class, either permanently or periodically, settled on the island.

They began to play cricket, a game that defined their social class. Thus cricketers from the plantation plutocracy like George Challenor were the first pioneers. But for cricket to become a viable game, they had to include a few Blacks, at first, to bowl at them. It was only a matter of time before a larger number of African-Bajans took up the game, for it fitted in with their character. Traditionally most Bajans, partly out of necessity, lived a disciplined life. Because of limited resources, they had to plan and order these available resources. This ordered and disciplined lifestyle fitted neatly into the highly disciplined game of cricket. But the African-Bajans soon began to transform the game to suit their African characteristics. Just like the African-American who took the Irish clog dance and transformed it into tap-dance, the African-Bajan took English cricket and transformed it into a game that was unique to them.

Again, cognisance must be taken of my uncle's remark: certainly Barbados and West Indies cricket did not begin in the 1960s or the 1950s, for long before there were heroes such as the Trinidadian, Sir Learie Constantine and the Jamaican Atlas, George Headley. These players were the fore-runners to players such as Everton Weekes. They must have influenced the Bajan players of the late 1940s and 1950s. Yet it seems apt to describe Everton Weekes's generation as the founding fathers of the modern Barbados and West Indies brand of cricket. It was during this period that Barbados and West Indies cricket came of age, beating England in England for the first time.

It was this generation that mentored the great Bajan and West Indian players—Sobers, Hunte, Kanhai and Nurse. Sobers and Kanhai, in particular, nurtured and brought on Lloyd, Federicks and Kallicharan. Lloyd batted with Sobers in India. This experience must have had a lasting effect on him. He witnessed Sobers' confidence and skill in mastering the Indian spinners. Indeed, it is

ROHAN KANHAI
Source: caribdirect.com

53

noticeable that Lloyd, when playing square or backward of square on the off-side, was a reminder of Sobers. Lloyd, the captain, together with these players, initially formed the nucleus of the great teams of the late 1970s, the 1980s and the early 90s; a team that included the great Richards, Holding, Greenidge, Roberts, Garner and Marshall. Thus, a clear line of succession—from Frank Worrell, Everton Weekes and Clyde Walcott to Lloyd, Richards and Lara—had been established. And this virtually unbroken line remained constant in that there were no pronounced dips or troughs that would indicate a falling of standard. Yet there is an on-going discussion as to whether the batting line-up of the 1960s was better than that of the 1950s or the 1970s; or who was the best batsman of them all: was it Weekes, Sobers, Richards, Lara or even Headley?

Let us start at the beginning, and the beginning, as far as this treatise is concerned, is the 1950s. This is the period when the West Indies team truly announced itself on the international cricketing stage. The batsmen of this period were Worrell, Weekes and Walcott and the bowlers were Ramadin and Valentine. It is of great interest that Mark Nicholas, commentating during the recent tour of Australia vs India, mentioned Laker and Locke of England and Bill O'Rielley and Grimmett of Australia as spinners who hunted in pairs and who were game-changing spin-bowlers. Not surprisingly, no mention was made of Ramadin and Valentine, the game-changing West Indian spinners that destroyed England in 1950; for the history and contributions made by West Indians are understated in such quarters.

Neither is it surprising that some West Indian commentators follow their English counterparts, down-playing the contributing role the West Indies played in world cricket, particularly in England. They have grown accustomed to unthinkingly repeating information from the 'Metropolis'. Despite this lack of recognition, it can be argued with some degree of logic that these players—Worrell, Weekes and Walcott—were the founding fathers of modern Barbados and West Indian cricket and these players were also pivotal in developing modern world cricket. It therefore, seems right to examine the career of Sir Everton Weekes since he is seen as a central figure in this dawn, for he can be considered an epitome of the founding fathers and a creator of the brand that is called Barbados and West Indies cricket.

The career of Everton Weekes mirrors the evolution of Barbados cricket. A book written by Weekes and Professor Beckles is a chronicle of this evolution. Every young Bajan cricketer should read this biography. Weekes clearly defined a technique that lifted Barbados cricket far above the English county cricket. Like the African-Brazilian footballers, he introduced a new science and an art to the game of cricket. No longer did a player wait for a long hop or a full toss to score, the method of 'hitting the ball on the up' (as the English now call it 'hitting the ball on top of the bounce') was being put into practice. Shots all around the wicket became the hallmark of Barbados cricket—the late cut, the late-late cut, the square cut even off the off-stump, the half-cut half-drive, the extra cover drive, the driving inside-out and the driving outside-in amazed the English players when they first saw Weekes. Indeed

EVERTON WEEKES
Source: espncricinfo.com

Weekes, in his book, stated that they were always questioning him.

My uncle, an ardent cricket follower until recently, spoke of Everton Weekes' batting. According to him Statham was bowling just outside the off-stump to a packed off-side field. He had no mid-on. Weekes, on arrival to the wicket, changed all of that. Using quick foot movement, he got right across, and, flicking the wrist at the point of contact, 'smoked' the ball through mid-on for four. Bailey, the English fast-medium bowler, was doing the opposite. He was bowling on leg-to-middle with a packed leg-side field (at that time there were no restrictions of fielders on the leg-side). Weekes drove him through the vacant off-side from off the leg-stump using a combination of quick foot movement and driving inside-out. Again, I am constantly reminded of a shot Weekes played at the Mecca against Hill, the Australian off-spinner. Weekes danced down the wicket to cover drive. However, instead of the ball spinning into him as expected, it drifted to the off. Weekes changed his shot, danced back, and late-cut for four. This technique of changing a shot at the very last moment is a legacy that has been passed on from Weekes.

It is noteworthy that on the 1961 tour of Australia both Sobers and Kanhai used this technique of changing a shot in 'mid-air', frustrating the admiring Ritchie Benaud. Any bouncer bowled to Weekes was dispatched to the boundary unceremoniously for four. Weekes' civility is unsurpassed. He is a polite and humane gentleman who is always giving pearls of wisdom. Thus the cricketing public gravitated towards this 'working-class' hero, and as such he gained many disciples who preached the cricketing gospel according to Everton Weekes. Consequently, many 'Weekeses' grew up across the island.

More than ever, Weekes' experience and method became the choice approach for all Bajans. 'Poking' became a term of abuse, while playing shots all around the wicket like Weekes was met with approval. To hook like Weekes was seen as a sign of manliness, a sign that you had become an African lion. From here on, this notion of a good hooker seems to have been embedded in the minds of Bajans. Hence, when Fredericks, Greenidge, Richards, Richardson or Best unleashed the hook-shot at the Mecca, the crowd erupted with roars that could be heard in the famed West African city of Timbuktu.

Not surprisingly, therefore, the hook became quintessentially or typically Bajan and West Indian.

It is of great interest that though the county circuit is said to be the so-called 'finishing school', normally English batsmen are far from the finished product, for it is very rare to find English players who have mastered the hook shot or even with the technique to cope effectively with the rising ball. Consequently, the bouncer is a ball that gives them an inordinate amount of trouble, and true to form, as already mentioned, they succeeded in restricting the use of this particular ball. At the same time Walcott, a founding father and a member of the 'Three Ws', specialised in driving 'on the up'. C.L.R. James described this shot in graphic terms—a good length would be driven 'on the up' back past the bowler like a rocket. Moreover, Walcott perfected the back-foot drive with a straight bat. He revelled in power-hitting. These characteristics of Walcott's batting also have been etched on the Bajan mind. Therefore when either Clive Lloyd or Richards savaged an attack in this manner, he was lauded.

Tudor was selected as a fast bowler for

England in the 90s. He scored 90 as a lower order batsman in one game. He displayed an array of shots, one of which was the back-foot drive, reminiscent of Clyde Walcott. The English commentator at the time described this superb shot as "very West Indian". Tudor was later quoted as saying that as a little boy, he used to watch cricket on TV with his beloved Bajan father. He listened to every word his father said while wildly supporting the West Indies team. This shot was the result of this tuition. Frank Worrell, the most elegant of the three founding fathers, perfected the late-late cut and a peculiar Bajan way of playing the sweep. He seems to have bequeathed this notion of batting elegance to generations of Bajan cricketers and spectators, so much so that Carl Hooper, the Guyanese batsman two generations after Worrell, is referred to as Sir Carl simply because of his elegant stroke-play. His average is disappointing, but this is overlooked by Bajans, for they only

FRANK WORRELL
Source: repeatingislands.com

see the elegance.

In a similar vein, the Jamaican batsman, Lawrence Rowe, scored a triple century at the Mecca, Kensington Oval, a decade before Hooper. The style, the elegance and the panache impressed the Bajans, for dull pokers who accumulate runs do not get the same recognition, and as such Rowe became a hero. A Bajan sports writer, Mike King, gave a graphic account of Lawrence Rowe's innings at the Mecca. He stated that Lawrence George Rowe was one of the most naturally gifted players cricket has known. At Kensington Oval, the local fans sensed that something special was in store when he reached 48 not out by stumps on Thursday, the second day of the Test Match in 1974 against England. On the third day, there was near pandemonium as nearly 20,000 fans broke down gates, seized every vantage point such as tree-tops and roofs, to see the elegant Jamaican play a masterful innings.

To summarise, Worrell, Weekes and Walcott were pivotal in creating a brand of cricket that is peculiar to Barbados and the West Indies, a form of cricket based on attacking stroke-play combined with style and elegance; a cricketing brand that is comprised of both science and art.

This is their gift to the world of cricket. In terms of bowling, spinners played a secondary role in Barbados and the West Indies. By contrast, fast bowling brings the crowd to their feet.

A local fast-bowler in the 1950s, Carl Mullin, was admired all over the island. Importantly, he is alleged to have had the most fearsome bouncer. It is said that the crowd would shout "skin, Mullin!" and he would respond by bowling a bouncer to the batsman. But the crowd did not expect the batsman to be struck by the ball. They reasoned that any batsman worth his salt and playing at this level, should be able to hook or evade the bouncer. This is all part of the Barbados brand. For the Bajans, the most thrilling sight was to see the Antiguan fast-bowler Roberts bowling a bouncer to the Bajan Collis King; and King in response, meeting fire with fire, proceeding to hook.

These cricketing experiences in the main made Barbados the centre of cricket. Such experiences were replicated throughout the island and were by far the main reason for Barbados and West Indies dominance, the other reason possibly being the competitive inter-regional cricket. But this inter-regional competition would appear to be the final examination which the Bajans had to pass, having already attended 'finishing schools' in Barbados—the village academies and the BCA clubs were such 'finishing schools'. In short, the inter-regional competition appears not to be the central reason for the rise of Barbados cricket. The cause lies closer to home.

In creating and promoting the Barbados cricket brand, Sobers, Nurse and Hunte closely followed in the footsteps of the founding fathers. They took the baton from Worrell, Weekes and Walcott, while Wes Hall and Charlie Griffith took the bowling baton from the lesser publicised Bajan fast-bowlers Martindale, Herman Griffith and Frank King. Enough has been said about Sobers and Nurse, so allow me to write a few lines on Hunte. He graduated from the cricket academy in Belleplaine, one of the strongest BCL teams in the North-East. Under the tutelage of Sir Everton Weekes, he mastered his craft. He cut and hooked by just getting into position and using his wrist. The first ball of a Test Match from any fast-bowler, slightly short outside the off-stump, was cut for four. He perfected the drive off the back-foot just forward of square to the out-swinger that began to swing slightly too early.

A conversation with the popular entertainer and calypso singer, McDonald Blenman, also known as 'Grynner', should shed some light on how Hunte and his generation kept the Barbados brand alive. Grynner waxed lyrically about Hunte's batting. He said he saw Hunte walked stylishly to the wicket in a Test Match. The first ball he drove elegantly square of the wicket. According to Grynner, that shot was enough for him; he went home feeling really good. But it is most important to note that Grynner stated that he was an opening batsman, just like Hunte. He played for a BCL team, again just like Hunte; the only difference being that he played for Victoria in Black Rock in St. Michael, while Hunte played for Belleplaine in St. Andrew. In short, Mr. McDonald Blenman completely identified himself with Hunte and his Bajan brand of cricket. Thus, Hunte was keeping the brand alive, unwittingly recruiting and inspiring disciples across the island.

This second generation of Bajan players who added to the brand were loved by the English spectators in the 1960s. Any Bajan living in England at this time would tell you that it was difficult to get into Lords or The Oval when the West Indies were in town. Kanhai, the great

Guyanese player who was nurtured by Walcott, added to this West Indian brand. Kanhai was a great player in terms of skills and cricketing craft. However, he over-emphasized the belief that he was there to entertain. No spectator could be bored when Kanhai was at the wicket. He invented his own shots. His trademark shot was to sit on his back-side and sweep for six. If Kanhai, like some West Indian batsmen of the 90s, had played for the sole purpose of getting a high batting average, statistics would show an average of over 60.

But Sobers and Kanhai, playing under Worrell, could not harbour such thoughts; it would have been seen as unprofessional. West Indies played to win and hence the players' gratification was of secondary consideration. It is noticeable that most high scores by West Indian batsmen in the 1990s accrued when the series had already been lost; when cricket was dead with a draw the most likely outcome; and most noticeably not in the second innings when most games are won. In short, the batsmen of this era seemed to play for themselves and to enhance their averages.

The Bajan players did not learn this special brand of cricket in England, for no fifth former (the English county player) can teach a university graduate (Barbados player) how to do advance Cricketing Vector Geometry; for this form of cricket was unwittingly based on mathematics—angles and velocity or timing being of particular importance. Again, it is said that the more county cricket you play, the better you become. This is a common refrain. Hence it is deduced from this that playing regular cricket on the county circuit improves the West Indian players.

Yet England has only produced two great fast bowlers, Truman and Snow, in the last sixty years, and no genuine great batsman in the mould of Sobers, Richards or Lara. Truman and Snow are the only two English bowlers that could regularly get wickets both at home and abroad. And most noticeably England, at present, is withdrawing at times some of their contracted Test players from the county circuit in order to address perceived flaws. This surely indicates that the English cricketing authorities have come to realise that playing cricket regularly on the county circuit, in itself, is not a 'finishing school'. Yes, playing cricket regularly is important, but you must play after practising the right method and this should be done at a tender age. In any case, constantly practicing at twenty-five can only marginally improve your technique.

Sobers had almost completely mastered his craft at sixteen. At twenty-five, he could therefore afford to sit around and play dominoes, engage in a simple match practice and proceed to score a Test Match century. He did not need the drudgery of playing county cricket all day and all night, for his cricketing technique by 20 years old had become part of his nature, like walking or talking.

This point of regular cricket playing in England has to be further addressed, for the advocates of the 'finishing school' used this as their central point. Using a motor racing analogy, Lewis Hamilton, the British racing car champion, learnt his skills at a very young age. Consequently he can do few practise runs and more often than not come out on top. Similarly, Bajans once upon a time at a very early age played all types of cricket, as Keith Simmons, in the capacity of the cricketing Nawab of Royal Air Force Rheindahlen, reminded me. Playing in St. James and at Combermere, he was exposed to all types of cricket such as marble cricket, tip and run, and beach cricket. He stated that he had a mentor, a West Indian opening batsman, George Carew. He also stated that at school he encountered a bowler, Bill Murrell, who swung the ball prodigiously. All of these Bajan cricketing experiences that influenced many boys of his generation, resulted in Barbados rising to the top. Hence on arriving in England, coping with the climate was the only problem he and other Bajans had to encounter; and not anything directly pertaining to cricket or anything to do with swing-bowling.

Finally, this idea that regular county cricket in itself was not a 'finishing school' is well summed up by a statement made by Dr. Sir Wesley Hall. He stated in his address at the Barbados Cricket Association's Awards ceremony in February 2015 that, as he recalled, the many times he was told practice makes perfect— one should practice the right thing because if you practice the wrong things you will end up perfectly wrong. In short, practicing the wrong thing regularly in county cricket is not likely to improve the Bajan cricketer. The 'wrong thing' is defined in this treatise as a fundamental departure from the Bajan cricketing brand built by the founding fathers. This is the brand bequeathed to us by Worrell, Weekes and

Walcott with the added features developed by Sobers, Hunte and Nurse. County circuit cannot be a 'finishing school' for this brand, since the two cricketing philosophies and practices are often at variance. County cricket is largely based on the Geoffrey Boycott method which is the opposite to Sobers' Barbados method. This is dour defensive play as opposed the exciting play of Weekes and Sobers. The Sobers' Bajan attacking brand, as opposed to Boycott's county brand, is a recipe for winning. This winning formula was as true yesterday as it is today.

Thus, according to Tony Cozier, a member of the staff of the 2015 victorious Australian team stated that "when the game's there to be won, it's generally the team that attacks the most [that] generally wins (*Sunday Nation*, March 29th 2015). The efficacy of this attacking cricket is borne out by the fact that between 1960 and 1990 the West Indies played eight Test series in England. They won seven and lost one. They lost in 1969, and in the deciding Test Match they played with virtually ten men. John Sheppard, their key all-rounder, was side-lined during the match with back troubles. This statistical information gives lie to the suggestion that "transforming the regional side from a dynamic group of entertainers to a potent strike force capable of demolishing any cricket team" began in the late 70s. Such statements as appeared in the *Midweek Nation* (March 18, 2015) seem oblivious, in particular, of Worrell's achievement. The success of Worrell and the raw statistical information point to a complete dominance over England and as such, the so-called 'finishing school' (if at all there was truly such a thing) could only have diminished the Bajan brand as opposed to enhancing it as suggested by the followers of Micky Stewart.

Thus the so-called 'finishing school', if it had any influence, could only have been an 'un-finishing school' on the West Indian cricketers during this period, in that it would have turned the team from an attacking unit into a defensive bunch; this is a recipe for losing. But the Bajan players of the second decade of the 21st century, unlike the generations before them, seem to have been convinced of this notion of a 'finishing school', for at present they bat all day against average or sub-standard bowling and can only accumulate less than 250 runs. For some unknown reason, the players of this generation seem to be products of the English 'finishing school', even though none of them have played county cricket; an amazing situation, for those that played county cricket in the previous generation did not seem to imbibe the notion of such a school.

This is self-evident in that all these batsmen of former periods hooked, cut, drove 'on the up'; they drove 'inside-out' off the front. They mastered the art of playing off both the front and back-foot. They remained loyal to the Barbados and West Indies brand. These shots have all but disappeared. According to Desmond Haynes, the present generation of Bajan cricketers are batting like Boycott and using Gooch's method of standing at the wicket and waving their bats around in the air (*Mid-Wicket*, 17 February 2015).

THE BAJAN BRAND AND THE SPIN-OFF

1961 was the pivotal year in which the Bajan brand began to be recognised by the cricketing public around the world. Worrell's team, playing this brand of cricket, was so popular in Australia that on one day alone over 90,000 attended a Test Match. At the end of the series thousands lined the streets to bid them farewell. Colin Croft disparagingly seems to dismiss

Worrell's team and their brand of cricket by stating that amidst all of this, they did not win the series. He is aware of the statistic that West Indies lost 2–1. However, he seems blissfully unaware of the reasons for this loss. It is important, therefore, to inform Colin Croft's generation of one particular blatant injustice which partly illustrates and typifies why the West Indies lost.

Sobers, in the third Test Match, claimed a catch off the face of Ken Mackay's bat at silly mid-off. This was the very last wicket and hence the West Indies began to walk off the field, claiming victory. The umpire said "not out." The game ended in a draw. No one should doubt Sobers' account of this incident, for Sobers, like Kanhai, Richards and Lara always 'walked', unlike most batsmen from other countries. In other words, Sobers always played the game with honesty and integrity and as such his account of the incident cannot be easily dismissed. This and other less obvious decisions militate against the West Indies winning.

Far too often such disparaging remarks are made by West Indian players when looking back at the generation before them. For instance, in the 1975-76 series in Australia, one member of the defeated West Indies team is reported to have said that the West Indies of the past played 'calypso cricket'. This comment, like Croft's, is meant to be disdainful of the West Indies team of the 60s, for calypso is seen mistakenly to be backward while, reggae and R&B are seen to be modern and revolutionary. This attitude typifies many Caribbean people. They are taught from a very young age to painfully reject their African historic past and this attitude of rejection spills over into cricket and as such they tend to dismiss the cricketing heroes of the past and their brand of cricket. "That's the past" is their scornful refrain, failing to recognise that these heroes built the foundation and left a proud legacy.

They seem unaware that their very existence is due to Everton Weekes and the many others that went before. They seem ignorant of the fact that the cricketing house which they currently inhabit was built by these founding fathers. Thus, they copy and listen to all and sundry, so long as they are not West Indian. Rejecting their history, they are left in the dark as to the role that fellow West Indians like Sobers played in developing cricket at home and abroad.

For example Sobers, as an adviser and coach,

accompanied the first Sri Lankan Test Team to England and now this team is rated far above the West Indies. They produce great batsmen generation after generation, and moreover, these Sri Lankan batsmen are not products of the so-called county 'finishing school'. Similarly, Gordon Greenidge coached and led Bangledesh on the road to Test Match status. It is ironic that the Sri Lankans and the Bangladeshis valued Sobers' and Greenidge's expertise, while Bajans and West Indians considered them and other heroes of this statue as relics to be forgotten, at the same time embracing foreign coaches whose track records seem to lack glitter.

In general, this rejection of their own history, while celebrating the history of others, has a deleterious effect on the body, mind and soul of the Caribbean people. Hence they are painfully unaware of the glorious tradition of the West Indies brand of cricket which, as already stated, is the Barbados brand.

GORDON GREENIDGE
Source: ice-cricket.com

This brand of stylish aggressive batting and hostile fast bowling was successful because it put the opposition on the defensive. The opponents sought to defend rather than going on the offensive to win matches. Moreover, comments such as 'calypso cricket' and other dismissive remarks demonstrate an imperfect knowledge of the history of the brand. In truth, it shows disrespect for one of the founding fathers, Frank Worrell.

Croft's comment sowed the seed for inter-generation confliction in that it pooh-poohed the generation of cricketers before them, and in turn has led to the present generation dismissing the advice of his generation. The trend was set whereby it is believed that this brand of West Indies cricket magically appeared from the sky and that there was just a cricketing void before the late 1970s and 80s—a failure to recognise that the West Indies were also on top in the 60s.

The comments of 'calypso cricket' and that West Indies were happy celebrating the loss of the Australian series in 1960-61 show an unawareness of Worrell's intellectual ability. He was a highly educated university graduate and a highly intelligent gentleman who refined the West Indies cricket brand in 1961 in Australia. His plans and methods were well thought out. Thus, in Test Matches to secure the gains made in the periods of attack, he often reverted to periods of consolidation. Hence Joe Solomon and sometimes he, himself, played a defensive batting role while Sobers and Worrell himself took on the defensive bowling role. This method and organisation allowed Sobers and Kanhai, when batting, to fiercely attack the opposition bowling; and similarly, in the bowling department, it allowed a rest period for the attacking bowlers, Hall and Gibbs, before they resumed the all-out offensive on the opponent's batting.

At the time he was short of an attacking bowler, having been unsuccessful in reinstating Roy Gilchrist, the extremely fast and fiery Jamaican. Allan Davidson, the spear of the Australian bowling attack at that time, spoke admiringly of this brand of cricket. He marvelled at the stroke-play. He stated he was amazed that when he looked at the score-board, the West Indies had scored before lunch what England had taken all day to score the year before. It is noticeable that when Griffith joined Hall on the following England tour, the brand underwent a variation. The bowling was continually engaged in all-out attacks, while in the batting department Hunte was used to anchor the innings even though he was by no means defensive, for he was a master of going from defence to attack; he had the ability to dispatch to the boundary the ball that was marginally over-pitched or fractionally short. At times, depending on the conditions and the situation, he struck the good length ball for four.

This brand ruled the cricketing world from 1962 to 1968. They sat on top of the world league table for the first time. The West Indies demolished all their opponents, including Australia and England, during this period. As already stated, this was the period when England came to the realisation that this brand of cricket was needed on the county circuit. Thus, in 1968, they changed the rules to recruit and accommodate the West Indies cricketing stars that sustained this brand. But this brand of cricket needs highly talented players and there were no immediate replacements, as the cricketers of this period were reaching the end of their careers. Consequently, the brand slightly faded until 1973 when Kanhai's team started to revive the West Indies by beating England in England.

Lloyd, the Guyanese, took the baton from his fellow Guyanese, Rohan Kanhai. Lloyd, unlike some West Indian cricketers of his generation, acknowledged the history of the brand. He publicly recognised the role Worrell played in creating this powerful entity or identity that is called West Indies cricket. In fact, wittingly or unwittingly, his plans, policies and approach were very much akin to those of Worrell. Under him, the brand became even more dynamic. Like Worrell, he stabilised the batting by using two players to anchor the innings; in this case Haynes and Gomes. In so doing he gave license to Federicks, Greenidge, Richards and himself, to attack. This approach made the opposition retreat as they wilted against this relentless stroke-play.

In one instance against England in England in 1976, Federicks and Greenidge scored over 120 in a partnership before lunch. His bowling attack of four fast bowlers created more waves than that of Worrell's and hence, more often than not, his all-out attacking method placed the opposition in an untenable situation. He thus made the brand more prominent and visible than ever, for he more than lived up to the creed of the founding fathers, a creed on which the brand is based—fast aggressive bowling and hard-hitting, stylish batsmen.

However, the popularity of the brand was like a two-edged sword. On the one hand it was loved by the English cricketing public, while on the other hand it created a form of resentment. Moreover, as the band became more powerful, voices began to be raised in Australia suggesting that a series against the West Indies was more important than that of England. This notion, if allowed to gain traction, would endanger the importance of the Ashes, the very origin of Test Cricket. Shrill voices became louder and louder against the West Indies. The West Indian fans in England made matters worse. Openly gleeful, they appeared to their opponents to be boastful. They referred to the English crushing defeats as "black wash". They rubbed salt in the wounds of their English opponents.

But the West Indies Cricket Board seemed unaware of the value that could be placed on their brand. The Board, like some of the present commentators who are mired in an inferiority mind-set, found it difficult to come to terms with the notion that the ex-colonial territory, the West Indies, could create something so valuable. Yet the evidence was right before their eyes. They saw, but could not believe what they saw. In Australia, England, India and Pakistan crowds flocked to see this brand of cricket. In Pakistan, they respectfully referred to the West Indies as the 'Black Wind'. In England, long and very early morning queues at Lords and Kennington Oval testified to the popularity of the West Indies brand. In addition, the television audience found the brand compelling to watch. This was not a drab and dull affair; it created interest everywhere. A visit by the West Indies therefore attracted numerous paying spectators and money from television rights. The coffers from the host countries overflowed when the West Indies were in town.

The Board seemed to have taken the attitude that countries such as England were doing them a favour by inviting the West Indies cricket team on tour. Like the followers of Micky Stewart, they saw the situation as England helping the West Indies as opposed the more credible analysis whereby the West Indies also was helping England. Here again the wrong analysis came into play: the cart before the horse and not the horse before the cart. Cocooned within this mindset, the Board failed to get anything resembling the full worth for their brand. These vast potential financial returns could have been ploughed back into West Indies cricket. This was a wasted opportunity to put West Indies cricket on a sound financial footing.

Yet this brand encouraged the English to recruit a wave of Bajan cricketers to England. Among the many second generation recruits was Ezra Moseley. This case study is of particular interest. His mother, watching cricket at her home in London, proudly announced to us that this was her son playing for Glamorgan against Somerset. We all shared Nooni's pride in her son's performance. It was striking that his bowling was causing Viv Richards some problems. Later, on meeting Mr. Moseley here in Barbados, I inquired as to where he learnt his undoubted skills in bowling. He told me at his local club in Christ Church. An Englishman saw him playing cricket locally and instantly grabbed him. He did not learn his skills on the English county scene, for he was an instant success. In any case the Englishman, generous as he may have been, would have had to be Jesus incarnate to pay Mr. Moseley a salary while he patiently sat around with the hope that his new recruit would quickly learn from an English master how to bowl in English conditions. Moseley, like his predecessors, already had the required technique to master the English conditions.

Again Moseley's case demonstrates, without doubt, that the level of cricket throughout the length and breadth of Barbados was on par or in some instances superior to anything in England. It also illustrates that the English cricket managers recognised this and went out of their way to recruit Bajan cricketers. This was to enhance their product by introducing the Barbados and West Indies brand. It was not to give these cricketers the wherewithal to improve their cricketing skills. In any case why would an Englishman be so generous to use their county structure as a 'finishing school' for West Indians who then turned on them and "black washed them time after time"? Moreover, the West Indian fans appeared cocky and in such circumstances; no opponent would provide a 'finishing school' to help the West Indies to win and hence to encourage this 'boastful' attitude to continue.

Butcher merits a more detailed consideration. Butcher was the first black player to play for England. There was a TV programme in England on this special occasion. It showed the background of Butcher, originating from deep in the pleasant St. Philip countryside of Barbados.

Many Bajans living in England were proud of his achievement and were delighted that one of them had succeeded. However, the so-called 'finishing school' clearly does not equip players to play genuine fast bowling, for no English batsman can master fast-bowling like Weekes, Sobers, Hunte, Fredericks, Richards or Richardson. Thus Butcher, without the requisite skills to cope with hostile fast-bowling, was caught in no man's land and struck with a bouncer, for the traditional English method of initially coming on to the front foot is a recipe for failure against hostile fast bowling.

Bill Athey of Yorkshire and England also played during this era. He epitomised this English method of batting and not surprisingly he also found it difficult to survive against hostile fast bowling at test level. In fact, the English commentators complained at the time that the West Indies fast bowlers were not pitching the ball up. Holding replied that he had no intention of bowling such balls so as to the give the likes of Athey free drives as they come on to the front foot. According to him, if they were desperately in need of drives, they should catch the buses.

Sobers' opinion on this pronounced front movement, even before the bowler brings over his arm, is of great interest. For him the ability to play off the back foot is of major importance. In so doing the batsman can hook, cut and pull. Moreover, it opens up the off-side to an array of back-foot drives. In addition, the back-foot play allows the batsman to evade the bouncer. And to repeat this ability to play off the back-foot is the traditional Bajan method as laid down by the founding fathers. In short, according to Bajan tradition, the ability to play off both the front and back foot makes a player the finished product.

The county circuit did not inculcate this method, and as such the so-called English 'finishing school' did not make the likes of Athey and Butcher finished players; the 'finishing school' touted by Mickey Stewart and his Bajan disciples had been shown to be a mere mirage. And by implication, it could not have been a finishing school for Bajans or West Indian players. Yet this case study illustrates that many Bajans, even though they were not household names in Barbados, had the wherewithal to excel at county level; certainly a testament to the fact that the standard of cricket on the island was already high and did not need an English finishing school.

The case of Gordon Greenidge some years before followed a different path. Also from the countryside deep in rural Barbados, he immigrated to England at the age of 14. He later joined Hampshire where he opened with the great South African opening batsman, Barry Richards. He must have learnt a lot from this illustrious partner. Opting to play for Barbados and the West Indies, he returned to his island of birth to qualify for the island cricket team. I met an ex-cricketer from Cyclone cricket club, the club from Greenidge's area in Black Bess, St. Peter. Here is this Cyclone club member's unsubstantiated account:

> "I visited Kensington Oval to see this Hampshire opening batsman that had lately returned to Barbados from England. To my amazement, when I saw Greenidge, I realised that he was Cuthbert Lavine who had left Barbados at a young age. I said to Cuthbert that his method had to change to accommodate Barbados conditions. Your trigger movement against fast bowling

must be back and then you can easily come forward when the ball is pitched up. The opposite movement is advisable for spinners; initially you can come forward, but you can rock back if the ball is short."

If this account of the ex-cricketer from Cyclone can be believed, then it can be safely deduced that Barbados had become Cuthbert Gordon Greenidge's 'finishing school'; the very opposite to Butcher.

PART THREE

THE WAY FORWARD

Any Bajan immigrating to England in the 1960s readily came to the conclusion that he was far in advance of his English counterpart. Hence, Cordell of Glamorgan, Butcher of Middlesex, Small of Warwickshire and Alleyne of Gloucester, unknown in Barbados as outstanding cricketers, joined these countries and became successful.

Gordon Greenidge is a special case. The question arises as to what made Bajan cricketers so special. Here, history and tradition became very important. The Bajans of that generation knew the true history and tradition of Barbados. Taught and honed their cricket at a very early age at the village academies (BCL-Barbados Cricket League) across Barbados, they had a confidence bordering on arrogance. Hence boys who had barely left school would confidently take on England in 1959.

Compare this with the false history the Bajan young cricketers are being given in today's world. They are told falsely that the Bajans were great because they perfected their skills in England. This message is psychologically damaging to modern young Bajan players. A notion is lodged subconsciously in their heads that the masters are in England, and that the Bajan must go there to learn and to refine their game. Hence, most young Bajan cricketers behave like perpetual students when competing with their so-called English cricketing masters. With such an attitude and mindset, they are bound to lose.

Compare this modern narrative of the 'English master/West Indian pupil' with that of Clyde Walcott's. In his book, he indicated that England was not in a position to teach the West Indies. This was in response to Hutton, an English captain, who was giving unwanted advice. As a manager of the West Indies team of the 1980s, he took the same stance. The English were insisting that he should play spinners as opposed to four fast bowlers. In the most polite language, he took the same independent stance as that against Len Hutton: "the West Indies will always play their best team," he said.

The way forward is a comprehensive action that mirrors the village cricket academies (BCL) and the promotion of traditional Barbados cricket. Gus Logie was part of the management of the West Indies A-Team that went to England in the very early 21st century. I went to Somerset to see them play. Logie, a Trinidadian and a true gentleman, stopped to talk to me because he was glad to see a West Indian spectator in the heart of the West Country. He stated that there was an important and continuing discussion among West Indians as to whether West Indies should retain their traditional method or change to a different style that is seen as more modern.

My cousin Vernon Hinds-Edwards, who is far more knowledgeable than I am, has no doubt about the answer. He is from a generation where the average Bajan knew the game 'inside-out'. He stated that the foreign concept of West Indies bowlers merely concentrating on line and length is destroying the game. He contrasted this to the bowling of Charlie Griffith. As he saw it, Griffith had a stock ball, but he varied his line and length (around that stock ball) as his main strategy. Hence in one instance he would bowl a yorker right up in the block-hole and in the same over give the batsman an unexpected bouncer. His intention, more often than not, was to make the batsman play, and to ensure that his bowling was unpredictable. Thus it was difficult for the batsman to settle in the sense that he never knew what Griffith had up his sleeves. Consequently, he often attacked the stumps relentlessly with his full bowling armoury.

On interviewing Griffith, he stated that by and large the above-described method is only partly true. However, he also stated that he did assess batsmen individually and if the wicket was lacking in pace, he would modify the 'Griffith standard method'. Thus as a fall-back position, when there was no other choice, he bowled 'line and length'. He left me with no doubt that his usual or standard method was to attack the batsman—all opposing batsmen regardless of class, colour or creed had but a short time at the wicket as far as he was concerned. Every trick in the book was used—delivering wide on the crease and then from close to the wicket, or advancing down the wicket to remind the batsman that the bouncer would come at a time unknown, or bowling medium-fast and then unexpectedly slipping in his fastest ball.

This is in contrast to the English method of just bowling and line length, which is basically containment. This method has become a West

Indian method—bowling maidens seem to be the only consideration. Thus, 2 for 90 off 50 overs is seen as an excellent figure. But no 'line and length' bowling can be relied upon to win Test Matches.

My cousin, who immigrated to England in the early 60s, is also sceptical of the West Indies commentators who constantly talk about reading from the bowlers' hand as to whether the ball is an off-break, a googly, a leg-break, china-man, etc. He argued, rightly or wrongly, that even the bowler is not certain that the ball will do what he intended it to do in the first place. Neither is the batsman certain of the line of the ball, for on delivery it might start on one line and end up on another by the time it reaches the batsman.

My cousin, who picked up cricket from the elders in the village and by watching the likes of J.K. Holt, states that the traditional Bajan way (as opposed to this English way of determining the type of delivery by just reading from the bowler's hand) first of all, is to pick the length early and by so doing you could come right forward and kill or negate any turn or right back with the back foot almost touching the stumps, and from this position watch the direction in which the ball turns. He argued convincingly that though you might have an idea which way the ball will turn, you must watch the ball closely, on to the bat. Hence Weekes, Sobers and Kanhai, all great players, by watching the ball closely, sometimes changed their shots in 'mid-air' when the ball did something different to what they had first anticipated.

Lawrence Rowe, whom it is said Bajan fans couldn't get enough of, seems to agree that picking the length early is the first priority, and this is fundamental to success. Having done so, the batsman's mind is now free to watch for just the lateral and vertical movement of the ball and play accordingly. Rowe is quoted as saying "people like myself, Viv Richards and Alvin Kallicharran could play off both front and back foot, and we picked the length of the ball much earlier than most." In short, Rowe is supporting

LAWRENCE ROWE
Source: sundayobserver.lk

my cousin's notion of foremost picking up the length of the ball early before any other consideration.

The so-called 'finishing school' for the modern Bajan player is nothing more than an 'un-finishing school', according to students of the game of cricket like my cousin. This for him can only mean going to England at an early age and learning how to plunk the front foot long before the bowler brings over his hand. This is the opposite to that of Sobers and Kanhai. Hence, to send a Bajan schoolboy player unsupervised to England before he has mastered the basic Bajan cricketing skills and before he has reached a level of maturity, is tantamount to teaching him to frown on this traditional approach and in so doing invite him to reject the great West Indian players of the past. No wonder the modern Bajan player turns a deaf ear to these cricketing heroes whose methods he sees as rooted in the past and therefore of no benefit in the modern world.

The layman, like my cousin, wonders how a young Bajan batsman without the maturity or requisite skills can be sent abroad to gain experience. In other words, it is like sending an infant abroad to learn how to run when in fact he is at the point of learning how to walk. He argues convincingly that without these skills and experience fostered at home the player cannot benefit from this overseas experiences. As an analogy, no first-form students can benefit from a fifth-form experience. How then can a 'first-form' cricketer without the required technique gain significantly by attending a cricketing institution or college in England? Moreover, the question has to be asked as to whether these cricketing academies in England to which these students are being sent have track records of producing great cricketers. After all, no astute father would choose to send his son to England to attend a school or a college that does not have an outstanding national record or more importantly an internationally recognised status. In any case, this period spent abroad can be seen as a time of no significant or visible progress, and as such a wasted period at this crucial stage when rapid development normally takes place. In short, this period abroad can be seen as a wasted interlude in which the time could have been used more productively in Barbados.

It is claimed such an English placement encompasses a whole package whereby the

Bajan cricketer, in addition to getting English experience, is given a good education. But these advocates fail to define what is meant by a 'good education', for a good American education is not necessarily a good German education. Education philosophers are aware that a major part of any education system is that of creating a desired mindset, a particular attitude, a way of thinking and a way of behaving. Thus, the American education system would tend to Americanise the student while the German, likewise, is designed to enable students to soak up German culture, heritage and to think and behave like a German. In short, sending a yet to mature young Bajan student-cricketer to an English cricketing school would tend to create a cricketer with an English taste and very likely a loyalty to England and its cricketing methods, and these methods are not necessarily the same as those of the Bajan's. Hence there is a distinct possibility that the cricketer will only return to Barbados for brief visits for his mind, body and soul would tend to be lodged in this his newly adopted country's social environment. He would tend to prefer remaining in his 'new country'.

Not surprisingly, many countries make sure

that any student going abroad to be educated has a contract to ensure his return. If he returns permanently, it is sometimes doubtful if this 'educated' cricketer can have a total commitment to Barbados' traditional form of cricket. Moreso, such a cricketer schooled in England could easily reject his immediate family; this is an education of social alienation.

Professor Chancellor Williams, in his book *The Destruction of Black Civilisation*, clearly described how such education can create an unbridgeable gap between the student and his family. He stated that "JL, a young Englishman in my college Oxford (Lincoln), who was one of my close friends there, refused to go home any of the long vacation breaks because to quote him, *'I can no longer associate with my family and old friends. I wouldn't know how to talk to them. We have nothing in common now, you know';...* Africans from the continent and elsewhere who, unlike JL, came from the privileged class at home... studying in England became more British than the British, just as many from what was French West Africa became more French than the Frenchmen."

It is not surprising, therefore, that a number of these Bajan scholarship students disappeared from the radar and their names are no longer mentioned in Bajan cricketing circles. And again not surprisingly, no young Australian or English cricketer was sent to a Barbados school during the long period of West Indies cricket dominance. These countries seem to have recognised the psychological impact of such a policy. Such a policy would imply that the West Indies were the teachers or masters who should be 'worshipped' and this could lay the seeds for an ongoing inferiority complex among the next generation of their test players.

The answer is clear. Teach the cricketers here in Barbados. Copy the Jamaican approach to athletics. They kept Bolt and other athletes at home and the rest is history. Give thanks to the benefactors of these scholarships, but make a suggestion that the said funds could go towards their cricket education here in Barbados. This 'under-20 stay at home' policy would result in recognising and acquiring the professional services of traditional Bajan coaches such as Richard Straker. Consequently, this 'stay at home policy' would help to enable the young Bajan cricketer to return to the old traditional Bajan way of playing cricket. Occupying the crease is not part of that tradition. Of course, a Bajan batsman should be able to defend his wicket just like a carpenter is expected to be able to use a saw and hammer. But no one would hire a carpenter on this basis alone and neither should a batsman who defends his stump but pushes back full tosses and half-volleys be considered a competent Test Match player.

Sobers once referred to this method as "just surviving"; good batsmen or great batsmen don't just survive. Praising the occupation of the crease, or in other words commending the 'just-surviving approach', shows how far Barbados cricket has fallen and with this fall only the bare minimum now is expected. In the past, pushing back half-volleys or not picking up the length and playing accordingly would have been frowned upon. Evidence that this low or mediocre standard is now seen as normal lies in the fact that an average county team visiting Barbados can beat a select island team and this is seen as the natural order; it is considered that this was always the case.

PART 4

PROFESSIONALISM AND WEST INDIES CRICKET

The Bajan disciples and followers of Mickey Stewart maintain that the West Indies players gained professionalism in county cricket. These advocates are yet to define their concept of being a professional. To seek clarity as to what is professionalism in Bajan terms, I spoke at length with my brother Glindon (Zaddules); he has lived here in Barbados all his life except for three years when he was studying at Mona Campus in Jamaica. He believes that professionalism, according to Bajans, means that in England you have to get up out of bed and go to work, playing cricket; it means playing cricket regardless of your feelings; for being paid requires the cricketer to do an honest day's work. But this idea of English discipline and professionalism surfaced from time to time during the West Indies dominance between 1960 and 1990.

The English slow and tedious batting was often

attributed to their professional and disciplined approach as opposed to the West Indies so-called cavalier and calypso attitude which on a whole trumped the English 'professionalism' before the West Indian cricketers ever dreamt of playing county cricket. So much so that they beat England 3–1 in 1963 and again 3–1 in 1966. It is of great interest that one English writer scathingly responded by stating that this 'English professionalism' was a euphemism for managed boredom—the uniformity of county cricket had dulled the senses and enthusiasm.

Yet any astute manager knows that to love and enjoy doing a task, be it sport or work, is the key to success. Thus the passionate love of Barbados and the West Indies for the game of cricket easily resulted in a form of professionalism. In short, the love of the game was the driving force that gave them the desire to practise and to keep fit. In so doing they maximised and show-boated their skills. This enthusiasm and love of the game together with the pride in wearing the badge and the colours of Barbados or the West Indies were the motivating forces. Hence, in Worrell's team followed by Lloyd's, professionalism took on a wider meaning.

The West Indies team, under Clive Lloyd,

had a professional set-up long before England. In fact, Gooch, in 1990 before the tour to the West Indies, set about to introduce an element of professionalism to the English set-up for the first time. Out went Gower who was seen as too laid back. A training programme was implemented. The players were placed in a camp to prepare for the West Indies tour. Gooch, the new taskmaster, was unwittingly stating that the English set-up lacked professionalism. This training programme mirrored the West Indies professional approach. It is ironic, therefore, to suggest that the English county system led to the professionalism of the West Indies team when in fact their national team lacked these qualities at the time and long after the West Indies had set up a professional structure at the Test Match level. Thus, it is not far-fetched to

CLIVE LLOYD
Source: unknown

suggest that the West Indies taught England a lesson in professionalising their national cricket team.

But, undoubtedly, the West Indies cricketers of the 70s and 80s were very professional. Suppose, as I am arguing, that this professionalism did not come from playing in England; what, therefore, is its origin? The Packer Series hardened the West Indian cricketers. After the first defeat, Packer entered the dressing room. He bluntly told them that he paid them good money to play proper cricket and that he would put them on a plane back to the Caribbean if they did not shape up. They did shape up by introducing a professional fitness instructor to ensure full preparedness for the rest of Packer Series, and this arrangement was carried over to the West Indies Test Matches that followed.

An Australian trainer/physio, Dennis Waight, was placed at the helm of a fitness programme. According to Tony Cozier, his strict methods, imported from rugby league, entailed distance running and punishing exercise, rather than gym work. He reasoned that cricket is a game played on grass. You run on grass and this you cannot do in a gym. He set the players a daily regimen of 500 push-ups and pressed them to jog miles uphill. Lloyd and his men quickly appreciated the resulting upgrading of their stamina, the decrease in muscular injuries and their sharpness in the field. To augment this fitness regime and at the same time to enhance the notion of professionalism, rules were enforced to make sure that there was adequate rest during Test Matches. Hence, players had to be in their hotel rooms by a certain time.

Viv Richards stated that English players ate "too much fish and chips." This statement suggests that he and his fellow West Indian players were keenly aware that diet was important in any fitness programme. They also, like the Worrell's team before them, employed highly skilled specialist fielders; Greenidge, Richards, Lloyd and Garner formed a tight cordon behind the wicket while Haynes or Logie stood at forward short-leg. But most important, West Indies had a professional Action Plan, though not formulated and written down in the formal sense. It was more in the traditional informal West Indian way and as such it was transmitted to the team members in an oral format. In time the team members carried this plan and the team motto in their heads. Everybody understood what was expected of them.

As Clive Lloyd publicly stated, the main goal of this plan was to defeat the opposition. So humiliated was he by the Australian defeat in 1975/76 that he vowed to avoid a repeat of this calamity. The main goal or objective emerged out of this situation. It is important, therefore, to further describe this professional plan that was used to achieve the stated goal of winning and taking West Indies to the top like they were in the period, 1962 to 1968.

Firstly, Lloyd recreated a pride in the West Indies brand. The four-pronged fast-bowling attack, efficient fielders, the fitness programmes, the curfews during Test Matches, were also part of the plan to achieve the final objective of taking West Indies to the top. In short, Lloyd's team adhered to most of the tenets of professionalism and it was a decade before the English team followed suit. The question that has to be answered is this: Why if the English county system was so professional was it not reflected at the national level, or if their system was so professional why did they continually lose on home ground to the West Indies between 1960 and 1990?

But it is important to remember my uncle's

truism: "West Indies cricket did not start in the 1970s, 60s or 50s." Hence the professionalisation of the West Indies cricket did not start with Lloyd. He only added certain features to this process. Professionalism was evidently part of Worrell's set-up. To get a first-hand insight of Worrell's arrangement, I undertook an interview with a member of Worrell's team, Charles Christopher Griffith, better known as Charlie to his friends. Griffith was a key member of Frank Worrell's team that defeated England in 1963. He took 32 wickets in the five-Test Match series at 16 runs per wicket. In short, he took 35 percent of the wickets.

Hall and Griffith opened the bowling at Lords in 1963 against the opening batsmen of England, Bill Edrich and Micky Stewart. The display of this bowling attack showed a high level of professionalism. There was obviously a plan—specialist fielders in place, each bowler had a role and most important, the bowlers were fit in body, soul and mind. To the delight of the West Indians in the crowd at Lords, Hall and Griffith were 'too hot to handle'. The bowling was fast and on target as the English batsmen jumped around like a cat on a hot tin-roof. In no time the opening batsmen were back in the pavilion. The question arises as to why the team appeared so professional to a West Indian supporter looking on from the outside at Lords. C.C. Griffith's interview gave an insight and thus provided an answer.

Firstly, the West Indies brand, similar to Lloyd's period, was very important to the players. Hence Mr. Griffith said he wanted to win for the West Indians in England, for a number of them were sitting on the mound at Lords. "I saw them there," he said, "and that inspired me." In addition, according to him, I had to win for all those people back home in the Caribbean. In other words, pride in the brand that represented the Caribbean people was the motivating force for the players, and this pride was an important feature Worrell's professional outfit. Worrell and his team were acutely aware that pride in the brand is an important and essential part of any professional organisation. Coupled with this is the fact that the team was well organised, another hallmark of a professional set-up.

The fitness of the players, their tough mental approach and the will to win, also inherent and important features of professionalism, were evident to their dedicated followers. In terms of the positive mental approach, Mr. Griffith said that in Barbados you had to be tough to survive in cricket; the game was very competitive at all levels and only the mentally strong survived at the top. But the very fact of being a black man, playing a game dominated by the white plutocracy in BCA First Division made you tough. He vehemently stated that as a result of this experience, when he was bowling he did not care about the batsman's race or social class. He had only one aim in mind: to send them all back to the pavilion instantly.

With regard to physical fitness, it was taken for granted that the bowlers took professional responsibility for their health and wellness. Thus, he used to get up at about three o'clock on mornings and go for long runs. (Here it should be noted that during Clive Lloyd's tenure there was a more collective and comprehensive fitness plan; all players had to buy into this plan and as such it was more advanced). His diet consisted of all natural and organic food. He ate yams, cassava, eddoes and sweet potatoes which formed the basic carbohydrate content. He also ate peas, beans and fish for proteins while he consumed local fruits for vitamins. It all gave him energy and strength. He mused that in contrast, the modern Bajan player consumes 'junk' food. In addition to the diet and the physical and the mental preparation, he also had to adhere to certain rules during Test Matches, one of which was being in your room by eleven p.m. With a mischievous demeanour, he commented that some rules were made to broken, sometimes.

To summarise, based on C.C. Griffith's narrative, the West Indies cricket of the 1960s was professional in its broader meaning, for going to work every day to receive a pay packet is just a narrow view of professionalism. Certainly, no qualified manager would harbour the myopic belief that just by paying salaries would enable him to get the maximum output from his workers. The modern West Indies cricketers are better paid than the players of Mr. Griffith's generation and yet they produce very little in return. This is partly due to the fact that when the Barbados cricketing authority refers to English county cricket and its professionalism, they seem to misconstrue the concept as just being paid for doing no more than a reasonable job, forgetting that such handsome salaries can breed complacency and give the players the wherewithal to live the high life as opposed to concentrating on cricket.

However, Mr. C.C. Griffith, based on his narrative, realised that motivation is an important element in being a professional and without this, all is lost. Yet he recognised the fact that there is a relationship between pay and performance. Thus he maintained high standards to secure his place in the team, for by so doing he secured a stipend and got the opportunity to travel. But what was noticeable during the discussion was his love for the colours of the West Indies. He was wearing a 1960s West Indies cricket sweater. Indeed he was a professional, for he adhered to the main tenets of professionalism, that is, pride in the brand, loyalty and a commitment to the brand, recognising his individual role within the team, the desire to achieve set team objectives, physical and mental preparedness, the required body of knowledge and skills to achieve the team's objectives and the receipt of a stipend as a reward for fulfilling all of these conditions, particularly as a reward for attaining the set objectives.

In short, the advocates who maintain that Bajan and West Indies players became professionals for the first time when they joined the English county circuit are cocooned in a particular mind-set. They cannot believe that the people of the region have the wherewithal to create anything of worth or organise themselves to achieve certain objectives. But if this belief is generally true in practice, it certainly was not true in cricketing terms.

This belief has a negative effect on some Caribbean people. Hence, they always look overseas for angels or Tarzan to come to their rescue. So blinded are they that they cannot believe that Worrell and Lloyd had such capabilities to develop a more comprehensive notion of professionalism than the one practised in county cricket or by the English cricket team at that time.

THE FALL FROM GRACE, THE SOLUTION AND THE COMING REBIRTH

West Indies cricket, with its epicentre at Bridgetown, Barbados and its fort at Kensington Oval, came crashing down in the mid-1990s. So sudden and unexpected was this occurrence that it seems to have left the proud Barbados cricket public in a state of paralysis. The comatose and fanatical followers seem at a loss about the reason for the fall. Like sugar melting in water, the days of glory seem to have left little trace of its magnificence — no obvious trace to inspire the young aspiring cricketers. Thus they have no existing heroes to copy unlike those of the past who emulated the famous generation of cricketers that went before them. According to Desmond Haynes, now they copy the English and all things foreign. But often I am reminded of 'Slammer', the village 'coach' and cricket 'historian' who went to Kensington Oval, the mecca, and saw the Jamaican cricketing stylists, J.K Holt. He spent the rest of his days demonstrating to boys as young as ten how to play like Holt: 'back and across' and 'up and across' became his mantra.

Amidst this paralysis and comatose state, there are some confused theories as to the reason for this fall. But amidst this confusion, there is one undeniable fact: today there are few 'Slammers' around the villages to teach the young boys, and in any case the villages are disappearing. Is this the major factor that gave rise to the decline of Barbados and by extension West Indies cricket? Barbados is traditionally the hub on which the spokes of the West Indies cricketing wheel are formally attached and hence there can be no West Indies without this hub unless a new hub emerges to replace the traditional centre.

At this juncture again, ardent Bajan cricket followers must be reminded of the commonly accepted school of thought. This is a school which maintains that the fall is due to the fact that England no longer serves as a 'finishing school' for the West Indian test players. However, as clearly demonstrated, this school is based on a false premise. In addition, that narrative lacks coherence. This school of thought is, at best, confusing cause with consequence. In other words, Barbados and West Indies undoubtedly produced fewer great or good cricketers in the 90s then it did in former years. The result or consequence of this declining number of excellent players was a reduced representation in English cricket. The Mickey Stewart school erroneously presents the opposite narrative. They state that as a result of the reduction in English country cricket, the West Indies declined. They, in their wisdom, put the cart before the horse. It is therefore necessary to put forward, in its place, a more cogent narrative, explaining the reason for the 'fall'.

Wesley Hall, the great West Indies fast bowler, opined that in the 1990s "the West Indies fell from grace to disgrace." The citadel and fort, Kensington Oval, was attacked in 1994 by the English cricketing soldiers under the leadership of Michael Atherton, a product of Lancashire, a county in which Clive Lloyd for a long time was the teacher and master. The West Indies, under the leadership of Richie Richardson, had no answer to Atherton. The West Indian warriors were shown to be mere paper tigers. It is of great interest and should be noted that Richardson did not seem to see this defeat at the mecca as seminal. For him it was 'no great deal'. It would appear that the Antiguan did not share the Bajan pain and lamentation, for the ardent Bajan cricket fans had not seen the fort conquered for fifty years and hence saw this defeat as a bad omen for the future. They had grown accustomed to seeing touring teams defeated at this venue by both Barbados and the West Indies for half a century.

Contrast and compare this attitude of 'no big deal' with that of Alec Stewart, son of Mickey Stewart. The son seemed to have recognised the importance of this Test Match. He scored a century in both innings, stating afterwards that some people refer to him as batting like a West Indian. The son seems to have fulfilled his father's dream. Not surprisingly, the centre of West Indies cricket gravitated to Antigua. But like a globe without its axis, the entity that is called West Indies continued to fall. The new centre did not seem to have the tradition and the accompanying cricket structure to create a reliable hub or strong fort. Hence, the centre drifted to Jamaica and eventually to Trinidad.

To shore up this new base, curious decisions were made, one of these being to select cricketers like Lincoln Roberts to form a Trinidad nucleus for the West Indies team. Yet, the fall gathered momentum. The cricketing fans mourned and groaned as the cricket structure created under Clive Lloyd was dismantled. According to Tony Cozier (*Sunday Sun*, March 1 2015) the last bricks were removed from the cricketing structure in South Africa: "The end was signalled on the 1999-2000 tour of South Africa. Those who had come up under him (Dennis Waight) had retired and their successors deemed his methods too demanding. I realised the problem when I returned to the team's hotel in East London one morning and found Waight in the bar. At that time he was usually out conducting sessions. The manager, ironically Clive Lloyd, told him that captain Brian Lara and Vice-captain Carl Hooper had approached him to ask that Waight ease up on his workouts. Waight duly obliged."

Thus, a new generation of leaders were at the helm and they seemed to despise the hard work that goes with professionalism; a leadership that seemed to believe that life is a continual fete. The days of Charlie Griffith seemed to be in the distant past, for he represented a section of the Caribbean society who saw dancing and singing as merely recreational or just one of the many forms in which the people expressed their cultural, political and social situation. It was not the be-all and end-all for this generation; perseverance, tenacity and commitment to the task that were paramount.

In contrast, the cricketers of the post Lloyd/ Richards era seemed to adopt an attitude of gay abandon, for in fact after one particular defeat here in the West Indies, some senior members of the team were seen in the party stand. The players were conforming to the stereotype of the one-dimensional Caribbean man, a man who only likes to sing and dance. To the horror of the fanatical fans they appeared to be revelling in defeat.

The Clive Lloyd fitness regimen had inspired, according to Tony Cozier, a corresponding improvement through the territories. Panthers like Faoud Bacchus, Sheldon Gomes, Emmerson Trotman and Shane Julien were typical of those in the Shell Shield at the time. With these players no longer around as an inspiration, lethargy and the lack of fitness have taken hold. When preparing for a Test Match, the modern players, amazingly, prefer to leisurely run up and down kicking a football—anything for an easy life. The ardent fans are left to wonder as to the connection between kicking a football and the playing of cricket. They further wonder why footballers do not likewise play cricket in preparation for football matches.

From here on the West Indies cricketers began to carry extra weight in the wrong places. Thus their running between the wickets began to lack urgency, catches that should be taken are dropped and the fielding has become pedestrian and toilsome. Amidst all of this, the centre continued to rotate around the Caribbean and again came to rest in Jamaica. Here the policy of securing the new base was reflected in unusual selections. Similar to the policy of Trinidad whereby players like Lincoln Roberts were selected, Findley, the Jamaican, was selected to represent the West Indies—a cricketer who would have found it difficult to make a BCA club side in Barbados in the 1960s, 70s and 80s.

The West Indies was being spilt into its component parts with each territory vying for dominance. An English suggestion to split up the West Indies in their days of total dominance had come true. Mr. Pearce, an Englishman, correctly analysed the situation in a precise manner. He was a teacher in a London high school and a political activist who campaigned for the election of Dianne Abbott (the black MP of Jamaican roots), and as such he paid close attention to West Indies cricket. He said the following: "when the West Indies were dominant, it was difficult to dispute the location of the centre, for this central cricketing territory was dominating the regional competition. So much so that it was difficult to argue about the selection of these players from this dominant territory for they stood head and shoulders above the many." At present the traditional centre, Barbados, is producing no significantly better players than the other territories, and here lies the nub of the problem.

The decline continued, reaching rock bottom with only Bangladesh and Zimbabwe below them in the table. The cricketing authorities turned to foreign coaches, but with little success. They then recruited Otis Gibson, the Bajan, in their quest to remedy the sad situation, but with little avail. The West Indies brand had become sullied and a mark of failure. Some players were no longer proud to wear the badge, so much so that one player openly stated that his prime interest was that of Trinidad and the IPL. Amazingly, he was promptly elevated to the captain of the West Indies ODI team.

Meanwhile the traditional centre, Barbados, remained in its comatose state. As part of the solution, the authorities started to send young school boys to England to gain experience. This policy seems to be based on the enormous view that England served as a 'finishing school' for West Indies test players during the period of dominance. Not surprisingly, an erroneous concept such as this has led to a situation whereby none of these players of 'English experience' have made a great impact on Barbados cricket to suggest a return to the glory days. This policy of partly looking to England to solve Barbados' problem is a mistaken course of action, again reading the cricketing historical pass incorrectly.

Bajans were recruited to England to play cricket because they were exceptionally good and not the other way around. They did not become very good or great players because they went to England. A retracing of the historical steps should clearly demonstrate the 'horse-cart' theory as opposed to the 'cart-horse' notion. For instance, Trevor Bailey of Essex, in one of his tours to Barbados, spotted Keith 'Bama' Boyce and recruited him to play for his county. He recruited him because he was an exceptional cricketer. Boyce set the Essex County alight from the very start. Please note that he did not go through a 'finishing school' process, for he was an instant success. His skills already had been honed in Barbados. Boyce's popularity in his new county reached fever pitch, so much so that when Essex played at Valentines Park in Ilford, the crowds flocked to the grounds with their picnic baskets. It was a day out for the family.

Again, Fred Rumsey's tour to Barbados was an annual event. His comment at the time in a prestigious English paper indicated a belief that was directly opposite to his fellow compatriot, Mickey Stewart. Fred Rumsey put forward a narrative that Barbados cricket was of high standard, and well-organised in a comprehensive manner; so much so that any player with ability would be spotted and likely be invited to compete for the island team. He contrasted this with England, whereby if you did not attend certain schools and were not inducted into the county system as a schoolboy, you were likely to be lost between wide cracks.

Such tours enable English scouts to recruit Bajan players, for Boyce, the generation after Sobers, was drawing the crowds. The pickings for these scouts were rich indeed. English county cricket not only found proven Barbados and the West Indies Test players, they also found a number of non-Test recruits from mainly Barbados. The English cricketing authorities eventually seemed concerned with this trend and ostensibly changed the rule to limit non-English players. However, this new ruling did not affect the West Indies Test players as it did the non-Test foreign players. Hence, this is where the 'finishing school' argument seems to falter, for the West Indian Test players continued to ply their trade in England. The vital question therefore arises as to why did the West Indies continue to fall from grace to disgrace, even though the English counties supposedly continue to act as the so-called 'finishing school' for their Test players.

Sherwin Campbell, Vaspert Drakes, Corey Collymore, Tino Best, Christopher Jordan, Brian Lara, Nixon McClean, Franklyn Rose, Shivnarine Chanderpaul, Wavell Hinds, Richie Richardson, Otis Gibson, Dwayne Smith, Jimmy Adams, Carl Hooper, Chris Gayle, together with veterans Curtley Ambrose and Courtney Walsh, continued to ply their trade in England during the West Indies' fall from grace. Many of these players had undoubted talent, and as my cousin correctly stated, they were no worse than the Test players of the highly rank countries. One reason, according to him, for the 'fall' is the selection policy and the lack of management skills both in Barbados and the wider West Indies. To support this conjecture, it is worthwhile examining the selection and the treatment of a number of these players listed above.

Franklyn Rose was undoubtedly an excellent prospect, but disappeared off the scene and without inside knowledge, one can only assume that it was not for his lack of ability.

But great leaders like Sir Frank Worrell and Clive Lloyd were able to manage differences in the camp. The management of Collymore is a case in point. The great Jamaican fast bowler, Michael Holding, stated that when he first saw Collymore he thought he was the genuine article. To my amazement, I saw him bowling lengthy spells at Kensington Oval (he was around 19 years old) in matches of no real significance. Not surprisingly, his back gave way.

The lack of maximising talent seems to be evident in the case of Drakes and Smith. In one of the Test Matches Drakes was batting with Lara. The captain Lara was overheard on the stump microphone saying "you look good." Indeed Drakes looked good. His batting in this match looked better than the selected specialist batsman. Could not this talent be utilised to make him into an all-rounder? Another example of mismanagement is that of Dwayne Smith. He scored a century in his first test match. It is noteworthy that on TV, the captain pointedly failed to commend him, stating that his achievement was due to the exuberance of youth.

Such managers of West Indies cricket fail to

realise that many great West Indies players began their cricket by playing 'shot after shot' and it was only after a series of matches that they tightened up their defence and settled into their ascribed role—Hunte, Sobers (took over ten matches to score a century), Lloyd are a few examples. Smith was removed from the test arena and made into a 'one-day' player, and this is where the gross mismanagement undoubtedly occurred. He was made 'man of the match' in an ODI and promptly dropped after. He was allocated the spot of number 8. After the batsmen before him poked around, apparently to achieve good personal averages, Smith was sent in to score at an impossible rate in order to win matches. When he unsurprisingly failed, he was dubbed a hitter into cow corner.

In one match under Gayle, batsmen such as Pollard were out hitting or as perceived, making reckless shot. Smith was among the so-called reckless hitters; he was the only one that was dropped. It fell upon the Indians (IPL) to recognise his talent; no one could fail to see the untapped talent. But in his autumn or winter years, now he is being given a chance to open for the West Indies ODI team. But it is too late to develop his batting potential. Smith's formative and developmental stage has long passed; "for there is a time in the affairs of men when taken at the flood leads on to fortune." Is my cousin, therefore, correct in stating that mismanagement and selection policies are major factors in the 'fall' of the West Indies? Such conjectures cannot be readily dismissed, for what sometimes comes into the open suggests a basic lack of managerial skills.

There was a case in Barbados whereby a player was sent home for failing to sign for his kit. Any skilled or trained manager would have had meetings with each player to discuss overall plans and objectives for the team and at the same time inquire as to whether any of his players had 'concerns'. He would then closely consider the situation, for a few players did have reasonable grounds for concern— apparently the rule of two shirts and two trousers being enforced contradicted the rule book of four shirts and four trousers; and secondly it had financial penalties for what could be considered 'wear and tear', in that if the kit got damage even when playing for the regional team, they had to purchase a new set from their own pockets.

The manager would appear to have

approached the situation as though it was a boot-camp or even a slave-camp of the past, failing to recognise that discussion and 'ownership' of rules by players are vital in motivating a team; but such managers have a myopic view of discipline. Rules and discipline are important in any organisation, but these rules should be explained to all members with a formal built-in mechanism for change if deemed necessary. And most importantly all rules should be reasonable and based on natural justice. No rules should be enforced that go against the natural human rights of individuals.

There is a vast difference between a competent manager who believes in discipline and a dictatorial figure. Moreover, from the outside, the cricket organisation seems outdated. For one, the manager of the Barbados cricket team is also a member of the Board. This in essence means a possible influence in his selection to the job. This smacks of patronage and hence the best man for the post could easily be overlooked in favour of the 'insider'. This situation is compounded when it is considered that the organisation does not seem to have a policy of formal appraisal. Such a method of evaluation would use set criteria to assess the performance of the coaches, captain and the manager at the end of a defined term. Thus, they would be retained or dismissed on rational grounds and not mainly on personal whims such as "I don't like the captain or the manager of the team."

Another case, this time at the regional level, also suggest the managements, overall, lacks the requisite skills, and this supports the proposition that poor management is the cause for the 'fall' of West Indies cricket. In this particular instance, amazingly a cricket team was sent all the way to India without ensuring that the players had contractual obligations.

However, though it is the accepted wisdom to present a number of causes in explaining an event, this narrative will stress one overwhelming cause for the falling into 'disgrace'; this being the collapse of the epicentre, Barbados. And this is compounded by the fact that no other cricketing centre of merit emerged.

This approach or method in determining the reason for the 'fall', though it appears at first sight to be mono-casual, has some justification. Other factors have been carefully considered, and as such it can be concluded that the collapse of the traditional centre, Barbados, is the fundamental and main reason for the fall of the West Indies.

The demise of the centre, Barbados, is self-evident. The conveyor belt, producing great players, very good players or even good players, has stopped. The energy that powers the belt has been reduced significantly or the switch has been turned to zero. The Worrell's, the Weekes's, the Walcott's, the Sobers', the Nurse's, the Hall's, the Griffith's, the Garner's, the Marshall's, the Clarke's, the Daniel's, the Moseley's and the Best's are conspicuously absent. The fundamental reason for this drought is that of the rapidly disappearing villages that nurtured these cricketers.

The village was at the heart of Barbados cricket organisation. Every village had a team which carried the identity of that community. For instance, Belleplaine cricket club carried an invisible 'banner' that represented the surrounding villages in St. Andrew. Similarly St. John the Baptist cricket club proudly represented Holders Hill while Welches cricket club un-mistakenly was the representative of Redmans Village and Welches. Members of such teams were local boys and young men who played on the beaches, on the streets and on any piece of vacant land. They, as boys, played knee cricket, 'tip and run' firm and all variations of cricket.

They played all day and every day. While playing, they copied their heroes—Worrell, Weekes, Walcott, Nurse, Sobers, Holt, Kanhai, Gibbs, etc. They fiercely competed with each other, often criticising those who 'cross-hall' (playing with across the line), they looked askance at those who played from square-leg (not getting behind the ball), or those who swiped (playing without grace or style). They frowned upon bowlers who bowled long-hops and criticized the batsmen who could not dispatch such bad balls to the boundary. But the political elite have found it fit to under-develop the traditional Bajan villages and as such the cricket academies are being systematically destroyed. The village communities were based on an African concept of living. Though the Africans, during slavery, were 'de-culturized' by design, elements of living as a community remained.

Professor Chancellor Williams, a foremost authority on Africa, described the traditional belief system of the Africans. According to the professor, Africans in villages and towns were classified into age-grades whereby the elders were respected. This was based on "the assumption that, all other things being equal, those who were living in the world and experiencing life before others were born should know more than these others." Such beliefs and practices were common in the Bajan village life. You spoke to 'Mrs. Brown' next door with deference and respect and she, in turn, could scold the younger members for bad behaviour. This is summed up with the African incantation: 'it takes a whole community to bring up a child'.

Land was commonly owned in Africa, and the produce had to be shared. Hence the Bajan village concept of sharing or giving to others and governing themselves were part of these communities, just like those in traditional Africa. Each village had an identity which they fostered and the cricket team was part of this identity. Hence a cricket match between BCL Belleplaine and Cyclone would be seen as a match between the villages around Belleplaine and Black Bess village. The people of these villages came out in droves to watch and to root for their respective teams; the teams represented and expressed the will of the villages.

However, the development policy of the political class wittingly or unwittingly channelled resources away from the villages and into new developments built on Anglo-American Christian practices. Thus, individualism and classism dominate the thinking that under-pins these settlements on the hills and terraces. The church organisation, whereby the priests live in big houses and whereby the seating in the churches give preference of the front row seats to the 'important people', are examples of this English-type classism.

'The rich man in his castle the poor man at his gate, God made them high and lowly and ordered their estate' is an English saying that is at heart of this religious practice. This is a far cry from Jesus' way of life. He dwelled among the ordinary and every-day folks and lived a simple life. Again, individualism is the dominant idea behind the building of these new so-called middle-class settlements; an idea lifted in all its form in particular from America. Ironically most of this social class in Barbados live on government patronage while looking down on the workers who produce the wealth. Not surprisingly, these settlements have been built with no provision for community activities.

Consequently, boys no longer play informal cricket matches; they prefer to sit at home and take part in individual activities like computer games. This form of development conforms to Margaret Thatcher's dictum: there is no such thing as a community. Hence, whereby in the past boys were lean and fit, today's generation has a high level of obesity; not the ideal for producing a cricket team. In any case, this type of settlement does not have an identity to produce a cricket team in its name. In the days when village life was a common feature of Barbados, boys took their cricket enthusiasm from village to school, played on mornings before the bell, played at lunchtime and after school. The games master would observe 'Agard' batting like Sobers and instantly draft him into the school team. And note that Agard had learnt his cricket in his village.

Contrast this with the present, where boys are encouraged 'not to play' for fear of becoming sweaty. All in all, this change of attitude and in the organisation of the society in Barbados has many negative out-comes. Bajans did not see it fit to develop the villages, as is the case in many parts of Europe whereby such village communities, systematically preserved, are seen as idyllic. Young boys who would once have been disciplined by the very organisation of the African-type village and who once played cricket for their village, now roam the streets getting up to mischief—even in a few cases shooting and robbing, or spending an inordinate amount of time on their cell phones. They do so under the erroneous belief that they are technologically savvy, when in fact they are in most cases just consumers of foreign goods.

This mirrors the situation in a high schools in London whereby students constantly disrupt classes with the use of cell phones, or use them to cheat in examinations. And as the case in Barbados, most interestingly, all the cell phones and computers are made in the Far East. When given periods to play games, these said London students have to be closely supervised, else they would rush off home to watch and play with their computers. This is in contrast to a school cricket match in Barbados in the 50s and 60s; nobody went home until dark.

The question arises as to what is the solution. The solution being put forward is based on the aforesaid analysis and narrative. In short, reconstruct the village-type organisation of cricket within all schools in Barbados. This organisation should be comprehensive and not divided up into fiefdoms between The National Sports Council, Barbados Cricket Association and school Physical Education teachers.

There should be some form of structure so that all these entities could come together and cooperate for the good of cricket. The coaches from these fiefdoms should come together to form a professional organisation to determine a traditional Bajan cricketing curriculum and an appropriate pedagogy. They should set out a yearly timetable whereby all primary and secondary schools would have sessions from these coaches. This professional body would have a system of self-appraisal to ensure that the standard of coaching is maintained. But most important most of the coaches should be transferred to the primary and secondary schools, for most effective learning takes place at this formative stage. But even more important, there should be a concerted effort to aggressively promote cricket in all the primary schools; instill a love and a passion for the game, while stressing the glories and international admiration that once ensued from this cricketing brand that is uniquely Barbados. It cannot be overstated that a passion for the game and a pride in the brand are the basic ingredients for success for out of this come the desire to train and to practise, the desire to excel. The motivation, trumpeted by sports psychologist, springs from this passion and pride.

Cricket sold Barbados abroad and is the only game in which they have been successful. All the other games or sport in which Bajans take part seem to suggest that they are there for appearance only and this 'also ran' hardly enhance the brand of Barbados.

PART FIVE

THE SOLUTION

The following outlines an action plan and a diagrammatic representation of the solution to the restoration of Barbados and West Indies cricket.

1. Promotion of cricket in ALL primary and secondary schools
   a) Take the Fontabelle cricket museum into the schools
      i) Create a mobile version of the Fontabelle museum with compilations of DVDs of past great Barbados players in action
      ii) Devise computer cricket games based on Sir Everton Weekes, Sir Garfield Sobers, Sir Frank Worrell, Wesley Hall, etc.
      iii) Design large, colourful wall posters of Barbados cricketing legends and place them at strategic locations in schools.

b) Give out rulers, exercise books, etc. all stamped with pictures of legends together with appropriate captions

c) Participate in summer camps

    i) Present quiz-based history of Barbados cricket (hand out the necessary literature needed to answer quiz). Give prize to winners.

    ii) Organise soft ball cricket - 'tip and run', 'knee cricket' etc.

2) Structure of cricket - Bottom up Approach (see appendix)

a) Coach cricket in ALL primary/secondary schools

b) Select the best graduates from these schools and place them in cricketing 'colleges of excellence', situated at convenient locations across the island. for example: The Northern College of Excellence (Alexandra), the Western College of Excellence (Ellerslie), the Souther College (Christ Church Foundation), City College (St. Michaels), Central College (Combermere), the Eastern College (Princess Margaret).

c) Select the best graduates from these

'colleges of excellence' and place them in a cricket institute (Lodge School).

3) Cricket Programme
   a) Revive Barbados' method of play
      i) Picking up the line and length early. Play back or forward accordingly.
      ii) Turn good length balls into half volleys by coming right forward or dancing down the wicket
      iii) Turn good length balls into short balls by moving right back and leaning back (limbo style)
      iv) Driving 'inside-out' and 'outside-in'
      v) Driving on the 'up'
      vi) Reintroducing the 'half-drive/half-cut', etc.
   b) Other parts of the programme to be devised by coaches at plenary sessions
   c) Appoint a mentor, a scout or czar whose business phone numbers and email addresses are made public
      i) The cricketing public are encouraged to submit names of young, promising cricketers, throughout the length and breadth of Barbados, to the scout/czar

ii) Thescout/czarwillassessthepotential of the players recommended by the cricketing public and accordingly ensure access to programmes. In some cases the mentor will act as a guide to these players

4) Teaching/Coaching Methods

   a) Coaches to convene a series of meetings in order to arrive at a consensus of best practices

   b) Coaches to convene plenary sessions to discuss the consensus of best practices arrived at in (a)

      i) Sessions open to fans

      ii) Guest speakers (i.e. Sobers) to be invited

   c) Final coaching method arrived at by combining (a) and (b)

5) Advertising and promoting the game

   a) Appoint an PR expert

   b) With the cooperation of school heads, use the schools' coaches to ferry students to regional and test matches

c) Create a special area in a selected stand (i.e. Greenidge and Haynes) for these students. Additional entertainment could be provided and during lunch and tea breaks.

d) Invite all BCA and BCL clubs to bring parties to regional/test cricket (a day out with mates)

6) Costing to be done by qualified accountant in order to raise money

a) Sponsorship

b) Raffles

c) Donations

d) Merchandising

APPENDIX

DIAGRAM OF STRUCTURE

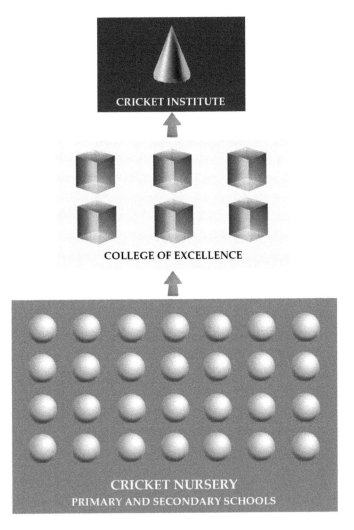

 CRICKET INSTITUTE 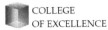 COLLEGE OF EXCELLENCE  PRIMARY & SECONDARY SCHOOLS

BIBLIOGRAPHY

Goble, Ray T.; Sandiford, Keith. *75 Years of West Indies Cricket*. Hansib Publications, Jul. 1 2014

Beckles, Hilary McD.; Weekes, Everton. *Mastering the Craft: Ten Years of Weekes 1948-1958*. Ian Randle Publishers, Jan. 8 2008

Drayton, R. "Britain Has Never Faced Up to the Dark Side of its Imperial History". British Guardian Newspaper, Aug. 20 2005

Fanon, Frantz. *Black Skin, White Masks*. Pluto Press, 1967

Garner, Joel. *Big Bird, Flying High*. Arthur Baker, 1st Edition, May 5 1988

Hunte, Conrad. *Playing to Win*. Hodder & Stoughton Ltd., Aug. 23 1971

James, C.L.R. *Beyond A Boundary*. Duke University Press Books, Reprint edition, Sep. 27 1993

King, Tony and Laurie, Peter. *The Glory Days: 25 Great West Indian Cricketers*. Macmillan Caribbean, Apr. 5 2004

Line and Length. Caribbean Broadcasting Corporation. Dec. 2014

Lister, Simon. *Supercat: The Authorised Biography of Clive Lloyd*. Fairfield Books, Oct. 1 2007

Manley, Michael. *A History of West Indies Cricket*. Andre Deutsch, Book Club ed. edition, 1988

Symes, Patrick. *Maco: The Malcolm Marshall Story*. Parrs Wood Press, Jun. 12 2000

Nation Newspaper. Dec. 25 2014. Page unknown

Nation Newspaper. Jan. 9 2015. Page unknown

Sunday Sun. Mar. 1 2015. Page unknown

Parker, Matthew. *The Sugar Barons: Family, Corruption, Empire, and War in the West Indies*. Walker & Company, Reprint edition, Nov. 13 2012

Pilgrim, Torrey. *The Sir Frank Worrell Pictorial*. Creativity/ Innovation Services, 1992

Scovell, Brian; Walcott, Clyde. *Sixty Years on the Back Foot*. Weidenfeld & Nicolson, 1999

Bradman, Sir Donald; Sobers, Sir Garfield. *Twenty Years at the Top*. Macmillan, 1st Edition, Jun. 1988

Tennant, Ivo. *Frank Worrell: A Biography*. Lutterworth Press, Dec. 29 2001

Williams, Chancellor. *Destruction of Black Civilization: Great Issues of a Race from 4500 B.C. to 2000 A.D.* Third World Press, 3rd Revised ed. edition, Feb. 1 1992

Williams, Eric. *Capitalism and Slavery*. The University of North Carolina Press, 1 edition, Oct. 14 1994

Lightning Source UK Ltd.
Milton Keynes UK
UKHW022118131119
353478UK00005B/231/P

9 781514 671047